The New
Authors'
HANDBOOK

Sam,

Happy birthday.

Geetha x

Other books by David Bolt

NOVELS
Samson
The Man Who Did
Adam
A Cry Ascending
The Albatross

MILITARY HISTORY ·
Gurkhas

THEOLOGY
Of Heaven and Hope

FOR CHILDREN
The Moon Princess

REFERENCE
An Authors' Handbook

The New
Authors'
HANDBOOK

David Bolt

PETER OWEN
London and Chester Springs

PETER OWEN LIMITED
73 Kenway Road, London SW5 0RE

Peter Owen books are distributed in the USA by Dufour Editions Inc.,
Chester Springs, PA 19425-0007

First published in Great Britain 2001
© David Bolt 2001

ISBN 0 7206 1011 6

A catalogue record for this book is available from the British Library

Printed and bound in Great Britain by MPG Books Ltd, Bodmin, Cornwall

Contents

Introduction

The Times Educational Supplement wound up an otherwise gratifying review of my original *Authors' Handbook* with the words: 'The only problem is that he is too nice; no eager author with an utterly dreadful novel will be deterred by his wise words from thrusting it upon unwilling publishers.'

My apologies to all the unwilling publishers; but, to be fair, of the avalanche of novel manuscripts (hereafter referred to by the contraction MS; MSS in the plural) descending on my desk since then, comparatively few have been dreadful. At least, not utterly. A goodly number have been eminently publishable, but sadly only a tiny minority of the latter have been accepted for offer to publishers.

My own first novel was published in my early twenties. I thought it jolly good – and still do – and so did a number of reviewers, but it would be highly unlikely to find a willing publisher today.

I will try to explain why.

Times change. After all these years as bookseller, publisher's reader, author and agent, I am still far from considering myself an expert. There are no experts. Faced with the constant takeovers and mergers of publishing houses, the fading of once distinguished imprints into the maw of the new conglomerates and the rise of unabashed commercialism make generalizations tricky. I can only lead you into the maze with some guidelines at best. A well-known publisher was quoted as saying recently, with wry, regretful cynicism, 'Literature is fine, but publishing is business.'

A distinguished ex-publisher and author advised that 'there are no rules'.

One can see what he meant, but there are rules of a sort and, while it's OK to break them if you're clever, it's unwise to break them from ignorance.

This new and revised edition is, again, intended simply as a guide to the 'rules', with the addition of some background to put them in context and, as before, some tips I have found useful – and the odd hobby horse of my own which most will safely ignore.

All the world and his wife, as we used to say, seem to be writing books these days; now perhaps read 'All the world and his or her wife, husband, partner or Significant Other' to be on the safe side. To use 'he' to include both sexes has been called a cop-out, and of course it is. If I cop out occasionally, it is only because the circumlocution makes tedious reading and murders the language.

The point is that publishers and agents get snowed under and are only too ready to dispose of anything that doesn't inspire. It may be lack of talent or originality. Equally it could just be poor presentation, an immediate turn-off, and this is what we shall be looking at.

Disclaimer*

Practically anything anybody tells you about writing and publishing will be riddled with half-truths, which is what makes it interesting. For a start, no two authors work in quite the same way. There are those who really need the quiet of a summerhouse (or shed) at the bottom of the garden – such as Bernard Shaw – or who rent an office, preferably without a telephone; those who scribble away happily on trains during the rush hour or surrounded by rampaging children with the television going full blast; some emulate Anthony Trollope who rose in the ungodly

---

* For the trade use of the word 'disclaimer' see page 113

small hours to pen pages and pages before going off to do a day's work at the Post Office; and some who run up the electricity bill throughout the night and descend at lunchtime the following day – being presumably otherwise unemployed. There are novelists who take ten years over a book; others again, such as Agatha Christie, who knock one off in a fortnight. (Don't be fooled by this, however; they've probably spent months and months on the preparatory planning.) I once assured a moderately successful author that he would do better if he wrote less and took more time and care. Wrong. The spontaneity was immediately lost. I remember one novelist who chipped away like a sculptor; having written some 150,000 words, he proceeded to cut it down to, say, 80,000. I don't recommend this approach, but it worked for him. Joseph Conrad reckoned that he wrote every single sentence on average two and a half times. This surprised me before I began to write myself.

The only sensible advice I've ever heard is that it's best to set aside a fixed time each day to write, to persist, whether you write anything or not on a given day, and stop when you could go on, rather than when you're stuck. But even that doesn't work for everyone.

Publishers don't work in the same way either. In most small publishing houses, and a few big ones, the editor who reads your book himself or herself and is enthusiastic will promptly come on the telephone or write with an offer. Simple. Most often it isn't simple at all. Many editors have first to sell the book 'in house', that is, to convince colleagues, an editorial board, the financial director and the sales force that he isn't out of his tiny mind; he's on to a Good Thing. This takes time, even when it works. An importunate nudging from the author might speed up a decision and bring the book to the top of the pile. Equally it might tilt the scales the wrong way, warning the would-be publisher of the aggravation he's in for if he takes this author on.

Also, publishers are people, with personal likes and antipathies like everyone else: something not always apparent from their catalogues. In my early days as an agent I offered a book on fox hunting to an eminently suitable, upmarket house whose chairman turned out to be strongly opposed to all blood sports; and one on birth control to an editor who turned out to be a strict Roman Catholic.

Not that publishers publish only the books they like personally. More and more it's unblushingly a question of what they believe will sell in large numbers – or won't. True, one publisher to whom I offered a beautifully written biography of an obscure – one could say unknown – character told me he would be mad to publish it as it certainly wouldn't sell; but it was so good he had to, and did. It didn't sell. But that was a long time ago. It could still happen, but it's a rare and lovely windfall in an author's life. I once had a letter declining a novel which the editor had enjoyed enormously. She begged me to let her know when it was published by someone else so she could tell all her friends to buy it. More recently I had a novel declined with the proviso that it would be fine if it were by an established author. A point I will return to. Catch-22.

You would be surprised to discover how many bestselling novels burst into the limelight having been declined by at least half a dozen publishers who didn't rate their chances or perhaps didn't like them at all. You can blame them only with hindsight – unless you're the author, when you blame them anyway. For that matter, how many bestsellers have you fallen asleep over yourself? Or haven't you on occasion greatly admired books your friends have never heard of? What sort of a publisher would you make?

I once assured a woman novelist that 'serious' historical novels were unpopular and very hard to place; which was of course perfectly true. She sent me by return a newspaper cutting with reviews of half a dozen just published. Just before *The Cruel Sea* came out – sometimes claimed to be the bestselling novel of all time – everyone was saying that books on the Second World War were finished.

If you disagree with any of the advice in this book, feel free. We are all in the trade working on the basis of educated guesswork, and we can all guess wrong when it comes to public taste. The same is true of any other trade. But an educated guess is better than an uneducated one.

Usually.

Can you sing?
Most people can and do, if only in the bath. If they enjoy singing, and sing a lot, the chances are they have a voice. Tone-deaf people tend to sing only when they must. Some rare birds have a natural gift that even without training can hold an audience spellbound. But it isn't the common lot for most of us.

Much the same is true of writing. Few actually can't. And if you enjoy writing, write a lot and can persist in the teeth of stupefying discouragement – which *is* the common lot – you probably have talent. But writing entertaining letters which your wife or husband, mother, aunts, nearest and dearest think marvellous is to professional writing what singing in the bath is to facing a sophisticated concert audience. Most of us need to learn our trade like any other traders.

There is a singular advantage for the writer, however: formal qualifications are far from obligatory. You don't even have to have A-levels. Admittedly the universities have produced some notable authors, but without stopping to think I could name a dozen successful writers who have had precious little formal education. One of the best is an ex-coalminer. Only if you are writing on an academic or highly specialist subject will the appropriate letters after your name give you a head start; but, even then, the want of them is a comparatively small hurdle which many have overcome without difficulty.

The writer, like the athlete, learns his skills by practising them. If he has someone alongside to tell him where he is likely to go wrong, and how to make the best of himself, that's the most he can hope for. The muscles are his own.

What this book won't tell you
How to write a bestseller
Books on this subject tend to be written by or about authors of bestsellers who had no idea they were writing one when they did. This *post hoc propter hoc* analysis doesn't work too well because, while it will contain interesting hints, it won't explain why the author's book became a bestseller when a dozen others as good, or better, published around the same time, didn't. Also, bestsellers aren't the same as puddings, and the mixture-as-before is unlikely to produce the same result. This is admittedly sometimes true of puddings, especially with a different cook.

Where to market your work
You should have thought of that before you wrote it. Articles, short stories and, to a lesser extent, books other than novels written solely to please the author may find a home if the writer is lucky or a genius. Otherwise the chances are not all that good. There are reference books which, if kept up to date, will give you the basic requirements of editors and others; but I don't want this particular book to be out of date in six months.

How to make money from writing
No one but a blockhead – according to that old know-all, Johnson – ever wrote for any other reason. A striking aphorism but hardly a fact, unless we accept as blockheads all those hundreds, perhaps thousands, of writers beavering away at this moment in the certain knowledge that they would earn more by the hour baby-sitting – if they ever get paid for writing at all. The desire or need

for money is assuredly one reason for writing, but it isn't the only reason and it isn't the best. In case that sounds lofty, let me assure you that a literary agent groans when a would-be author assures him, 'I'm not interested in the money.' The agent is. But writing solely for money carries the implication that this is not what the freelance really enjoys writing or wants to write, and this seldom achieves the best results. Writers of light romance, blood-and-thunder or, these days, not-so-soft porn may tell you it isn't what they enjoy writing, but they are either lying or deceiving themselves. Otherwise it wouldn't be any good. I'm thinking of a well-known woman novelist who spent years writing light romances until she had built up a name and a modest fortune, at which point she felt she could afford to take time off to write the work of profound and 'serious' literature she'd always wanted to write, only to discover that she'd been writing what she wanted to write all the time, which is why she was so good at it. The aim of any writer is to reach as wide a readership as possible. Naturally this equates with making money, but the aim is somewhat different. There are correspondence schools which teach you how to make money from writing, and so they may; if your ambition is limited to writing as a part-time hobby, join one by all means. But with respect, they are for the amateur; this book is for the would-be professional.

What to write

If you have an enviable track record of bestselling books – in which case you won't be reading this one – or are, as we say, 'distinguished in fields other than literature' – a film star, TV personality, retired cabinet minister or reformed criminal – advice on what to write might come in useful, since it's going to sell mainly on your name. Otherwise, you should write what you want to write *con amore*, within the wide choice of markets open to you. Professional journalists, of course, write almost anything to order and sometimes very well indeed; but this book is not for them either.

How to write good English

One bestselling novelist, in the course of an interview, modestly made no claims to being a great writer but rashly added that as an ex-schoolmaster he at least wrote good English. There, I said to myself, is a man who has never browsed through Fowler's *Modern English Usage*. If you would be grammatically correct – some would say pedantic – it is a splendidly salutary and humbling experience. Otherwise, rest assured that provided you avoid the more common and obvious solecisms, few readers – and, sadly, editors – will find fault.

What this book will tell you

How to plan and prepare your work

This is vital when approaching those jaded professionals – publishers or literary agents – whom you are inviting, remember, to invest time and money considering and, with luck, marketing it; who most probably face a pile of MSS like yours every working day and are only too ready to weed out those not apparently meriting serious study.

How to present your work

Publishers and literary agents get snowed under with MSS, to the extent that many these days insist that the initial approach should be limited to a synopsis and sample pages of text, accompanied by a stamped self-addressed envelope. Include a brief CV. They will then tell you if they want to see the full MS. Or not. With agents, this is strongly recommended; they may have a full list, meaning they will be severely restricted, but still won't ignore something uniquely promising for their market. Increasingly this applies to publishers, too.

What not to write
Some categories that stand a minimal chance from an unknown author, and why.

How to avoid bad English.
The most common mistakes made by ordinary people such as schoolteachers and those who write to *The Times* every day, which are acceptable in letters and business and advertising copy but which can brand the would-be professional author as an amateur.

How to set up shop
How to practise as a professional; how to work with an agent and a publisher; what to expect and what not to.

In brief, the book will tell you how to *get it right first time* and save yourself – and others – time and trouble.

Stage 1

Planning Your Work

1 Starting out

Look before you leap. Before a rider tackles a show-jumping circuit he first walks the course to see what he's up against. It's not a bad idea to apply this to writing.

Equipment – mental

> I had thoughts, ideas, but all fell on frosty soil, and a little sunshine would have been so helpful to me.

> I write little now. It is impossible to compose except under the strong assurance of finding sympathy in what you write.

The first quotation is from George Meredith, who went on to become a Victorian literary lion. The second was said by Shelley.

As a writer you are creating a product – in cinematic terms a 'property' – like any other manufacturer. Whatever is offered, from fish-fingers to ocean-going yachts, not everybody is going to want it or even like it. Creative writing is no different except in one important respect: it is uniquely personal to you. Every would-be author's typewriter, word processor, computer or exercise book should carry the warning: WRITING CAN SERIOUSLY DAMAGE YOUR HEALTH.

No, I don't mean chain-smoking or drinking or going without sleep or starving in an attic, or any of the other hazardous – and more interesting – things artists are supposed to do and generally don't. I'm not even referring to the dangers of asking your wife's/husband's/lover's frank and honest opinion of what you've just written and what this can do to your blood pressure if they are silly enough to give it. I mean the risk of associating yourself too closely with your work. I'm hardly the first to draw parallels between the average time taken to write a book – nine months – and the other, better-known gestation. The rejection of your precious child is taken as a rejection of yourself. Personally. Try to see this for the nonsense it is. It isn't easy. (It isn't even true if you have written your autobiography; but you probably shouldn't have, as I'll explain presently.)

Let's start with a maxim so obvious it's easily overlooked. The quality of your work is no whit affected by the opinions of others. Praise doesn't make it any better, and denigration doesn't make it any worse. It is said with a great deal of truth that a book review will often tell you more about the reviewer than about the book. Like all maxims, it shouldn't be pressed too far: arrogance is the front of a closed mind. A degree of humility is a bonus; Michelangelo was found weeping before his sculpture because he could find no fault in it, so knew his judgement was failing. But not too much either. A somewhat cynical bookseller remarked to me, 'The thing I like about X [a friend and well-known novelist] is that he's third-rate, and doesn't pretend to be anything else.' I took his point; and disagreed. Not every writer can be first-rate. But every writer should aim to be, in Browning's sense that a man's reach should exceed his grasp. Of course we're not talking about levels of literature but levels of professionalism. If you don't believe in your work, it's unreasonable to expect anybody else to. Fame, as Milton did say, is the spur.* Praise and encouragement is also a spur – few will disagree with Meredith and Shel-

---

* Disapprovingly; he called it the last infirmity of a noble mind

ley – but so is adverse criticism if it has an element of recognizable truth, however unpalatable, and it directs your attention to faults you admit and accept when you've stopped grinding your teeth. If it doesn't, ignore it. It can be the spur to improve, even start afresh, because books, unlike babies, can be remodelled and improved and even, if need be, discarded as 'prentice work in favour of the next.

Writers invariably start as readers. They aim to write the sort of thing they enjoy reading. This is fine and proper, provided you pause and remember that the books you have most enjoyed reading, perhaps some years back, aren't necessarily the sorts of books that are popular today – and also that you don't end up discovering you've rewritten a classic novel and not half so well. The point is, you have to find the buyer who shares your taste. Don't be too easily put off by those who don't. An academic I represented, whose scholarly books were selling respectably, mentioned one day that he had once written a book for children. I asked what had become of it. 'Oh,' he said, 'I sent it to Rosencrantz and Guildenstern and they turned it down, so I put it away in a drawer somewhere.' I said I had better have a look at it anyway. I loved it, and so did the first publisher I sent it to, who accepted it at once. Provided your work is produced to a professional standard, which is what this handbook is all about, it's a matter of taste.

It's a well-known aphorism that a writer needs two things: inspiration and the ability to work without it. The same is true of encouragement. You do need talent. You need faith in yourself and determination and patience, and you need to learn your trade. But you need something else too, though those to whom success comes easily will seldom believe, let alone admit it: and that is luck. Public taste is fickle, even ephemeral, going in trends; the most 'trendy' books are those that start a new one – impossible to anticipate.

When you have made it, try not to lose the precious gift of gratitude, not only to those ladders by which you climbed – those in the trade who needed you a lot less than you needed them; a position now inevitably reversed – but to Lady Luck herself, whatever name you give her.

Equipment – physical

According to the novelist Fay Weldon, 'All you need as a writer is a paper and pencil' – a lovely example of the half-truth. If you are starting on this perilous expedition, not rich and not yet calculating what you can claim against income tax on your literary earnings, it isn't recommended that you rush to employ a secretary or accountant. It isn't recommended that you use a typing agency either – which is what your paper and pencil must commit you to, unless you have a long-suffering friend who will type it for you, for typed the finished work must be. These good things will follow when you are established, but meanwhile it's advisable to take them step by step.

Dictionary

Personally, I'd put this as the very first of all the possible tools of the trade. Even if you can spell, there are surely some words you only *think* you know the meaning of. It's worth while making sure. Cultivate the habit of looking up any word you come across for the first time or are not *totally* sure of. A good dictionary will also serve the purpose of a thesaurus in suggesting alternatives when you don't want to repeat yourself. Any writer who works without a dictionary to hand is either a linguistic expert or very rash. It doesn't matter if you are a bad or uncertain speller, provided you know it – if you don't, no one can help you at this stage. If you are in the least uncertain of spelling or correct meaning, check. Nine times out of ten you were right first time, the tenth time will justify the effort.

Typescript

Many authors today have progressed beyond the conventional

typewriter to word processor or computer, but the basic keyboard skills are the same and need to be mastered. You will not only save money on a professional typist but also get a much better impression of what your work will look like in print. Many writers resort to longhand when they are stuck and are trying out variations; some may even feel a sort of mystic, intimate link between imagination and the act of writing by hand, but typed the final manuscripts must be. In some cases a disk may be acceptable, but don't assume that unless you are told.

Notebooks
Ideally these should be kept beside your place of work, beside your bed or in your pocket to jot down those precious ideas which come to you at odd times and are easily forgotten. Most will turn out to be useless – especially those that come to you in the middle of the night or after one gin too many! – but some will be gems.

Log books to record where work is sent out, when and the result – including, optimistically, payment received.

Work books. Anything relevant to the work you're engaged on: chronology, background, dates. These are especially useful in fiction to maintain continuity – how long, for example, your heroine has been pregnant! They can contain the skeleton of your work-in-progress and perhaps potted biographies of your characters.

Record expenses incurred in connection with your work that are tax-deductible: paper, post, part-accommodation if you work from home and almost all justifiable outgoings – as a professional author; unpublished authors don't count. So don't claim for your first typewriter or word processor, let alone computer, but only for replacements later when you are established. But a one-book author (autobiography?) would likely be disqualified, too, as non-professional.

Reference books
The Writer's Handbook (Macmillan, a hefty paperback) has a wealth of information, especially for new authors, including lists of publishers and literary agents and usually named contacts to write to; similar is the *Writers' and Artists' Yearbook* (A. & C. Black). You may also need books supplying the background of information to the work you have embarked on, if it has a factual basis, even regarding places, flora and fauna, etc. I have an invaluable one with twelve chapters covering the months of the year in England, and recommend something of the sort if, like me, you have difficulty in remembering exactly when apple blossom appears or whether you are likely to tread on a grass snake. Obviously if you are writing a biography, you will want anything and everything in print on your subject. For computer buffs the Internet is of course invaluable for fact-checking and updates; also dictionaries and other reference works are available on CD-ROM or online.

Dictionary of quotations
Expensive and optional, but invaluable if you are quoting a well-known phrase or saying from memory. If you get it wrong, it is not only disrespectful to the originator but irritating to the educated reader or editor, signifying that you haven't bothered to look it up. Can you spot the misquote in 'They shall not grow old, as we that are left grow old'? It is also a rich quarry for book titles, such as *Gone with the Wind*, *The Grapes of Wrath*, *The Houses in Between* or, more recently, *A House Divided* – originally from the Bible, another valuable source. I'm sure you can think of dozens more.

Maps and timetables
Essential if you need to get your facts right; for example, how long it took your hero to drive from Edinburgh to Woking or to fly from Paris to Moscow and for connections, etc.

Envelope file covers
As opposed to files, for packaging loose-leaf MSS for submission.

Punch
For making holes in MSS to be inserted in ring-binders.

Stapler
For attaching a limited number of pages (such as synopses) so that they won't fall apart and for attaching anything to letters.

Scrap books
For cuttings from newspapers and magazines which could come in useful or with ideas you can use. One can be kept for reviews of your own work.

Card index file
Useful, especially for non-fiction, if you need to keep a brief note of salient facts for future reference as they come up.

Wastepaper basket
Large.

Obviously you won't need all of these, at least to start with, and equally obviously you may think of more. But pick the ones useful to you.

2 Getting it right

When we first learn to play a musical instrument most of us accept the fact that we begin with no prior knowledge: there is nothing to unlearn. Our mistakes are going to be tentative mistakes, which can be corrected as they crop up – and before they grow into bad habits. This is not true of professional writing. We have been writing something most of our lives, even if only school essays, letters or diaries. When we come to writing for publication it is more than likely that closer examination will reveal all sorts of bad habits that need to be unlearnt.

Style

'Style', as Georges Le Clerk de Buffon remarked in the eighteenth century (in French of course), 'is the man himself.' No one has put it better in the last two centuries, and I'm not about to try. Style can't be taught, but it can be copied, and I will risk saying here that all writers begin by emulating, consciously or unconsciously, the style of an admired author. Indeed when I was at school we were given essays to write 'in the style of', say, Katherine Mansfield or D.H. Lawrence. I dare say today it would be contemporary authors (including some very dubious stylists, I would add; which is only to say that opinions are going to vary again). It wasn't a bad idea at that. It made us conscious of style. It may also have served as a warning to those of us destined to get involved in the business of professional writing not to copy too assiduously another's well-known style.

Style is nothing more or less than the manner in which the author presents his subject. It is no substitute for the subject matter itself; no substitute for the story or content. (To the poet, it's practically everything; but to describe Death as 'The undiscover'd country from whose bourn / No traveller returns' would look distinctly out of place in a modern novel.) Your style is an embellishment, the dressing-up of the body of your narrative, and it can easily be overdone, like the outfit of an over-dressed woman. If a woman is really well dressed, attention is drawn to the woman, not the clothes. Only upon reflection do we realize why she caught our eye. The same is true of a good style in writing. Nothing is worse than the patently self-conscious, where the writer or the woman is too obviously trying to impress. If style is the manner of presentation, then mannerism is, in the words of the *Concise Oxford Dictionary*, 'Excessive addition to a distinctive manner in art or literature.' (I give a passing nod here to high-fliers such as Meredith or Lawrence Durrell, whose style is on occasion better than the content and admired for its own sake.)

But note that 'excessive'.

New writers tend to be excessively conscious of style. The very best advice that can be given is: forget it. The first requirement is clarity. Concentrate on that. Your own, personal style will evolve as you go along. It's like handwriting, if that's something you care about at all. You begin by forming letters as accurately as you can, with the sole intention of producing something that can be read and understood. In the natural course of events it will change (and, if you care, improve), probably because you are now emulating the handwriting of someone else whose style you like. But eventually your individual personality will break through – ask any graphologist. The style is then your own. What is more, it will be natural.

In the novel, which we'll come to presently, the essential background information should ideally be introduced as if by chance, like the lovers who 'Walk down the street on the chance that they meet, And they meet, not really by chance'. It should not hold up the traffic. This is, if anything, even more true of style. It should read as if from your pen – or off your keyboard – flowed the first words that entered your head.

Of course you are doing no such thing.

It is a truism that can't be repeated too often that easy writing makes for hard reading – and hard writing for easy reading – and perhaps curiously this is particularly relevant to writers who have a formidable command of the language and are sorely tempted to display it – in other words to show off, a style known as meretricious, 'showily attractive', from the Latin *meretrix*, a prostitute. Conrad claimed to write every single sentence two and a half times before he got it right. The theologian and fine stylist Henry Drummond beat that. He reckoned to write every sentence three times: first in simplicity, secondly in profundity and thirdly in profundity disguised as simplicity. The result? It looked as if his writing flowed from his pen. For example, he wrote: 'To see some small soul pirouetting throughout life on a single text . . . is not a Christian sight.'* Simple, yes. But look at that pirouetting again. It's so much the right word, it has the appearance of coming naturally: flowing from Drummond's pen almost unasked. I bet it didn't.

To some extent your material will determine your style. A beautifully described account of the sun rising over Lake Windermere, in tune with the observer's mood and a carefully crafted way of expressing it (the mood), which might be a *tour de force* in a literary or even general novel, in a straight thriller could amount to no more than what is rudely called a 'purple patch': a vain showing of 'fine writing' (even if it is indeed fine), totally out of place. Like a white tie and tails at a rave.

---

* *The Greatest Thing in the World*

Let your style come naturally, decided by your skill in selecting the best – not the prettiest or most unusual – words to express what you want to say, or the fact you mean to get across to the reader, and the degree of originality you can, as a second consideration, bring to them without going overboard, bearing in mind that the pursuit of originality for its own sake is the hallmark of the amateur. Don't ever be afraid to use plain English.

Which brings us to clichés. A cliché is a literary novelty which, like many novelties, soon gets worn out. The language has thousands of commonplace phrases which are well worn but never wear out, which you can't possibly avoid using; but they aren't clichés because they never have been 'novelties', in the sense of attracting attention to their excellence and originality. The first person to coin the phrase 'a sickening thud' or to describe a road that 'wound like a white ribbon' over the moor or even made the jilted girl complain that she was 'cast off like a worn-out glove' deserves nothing but applause. These phrases are extremely apt. We laugh at them now only because they have become hackneyed; and they have become hackneyed only because they were so apt that they were copied again and again. (If you can think of phrases more apt to describe these conditions, you are yourself a fine writer; you may even invent a new cliché.)

Fashions do change, and I think it fair to say that the long-winded philosophizing of some of the Victorian novelists, admirable though they may have been in their context, would be calculated to put today's reader – or editor – off. Asides to 'the gentle reader' are no longer welcomed. Long-winded you may be, if it's relevant and necessary; but *relevant* is the key word.

It applies also to the apparent trivia: casual remarks like 'Mark put his teaspoon down carefully in the saucer.' Hemingway was good at this. Unhappily he has been much copied by writers who aren't good at it and miss the point. The action, however trivial, shouldn't be merely a substitute for 'Mark said' (see Dialogue on page 45). Not that it's objectionable; but it shouldn't be used too often. It ought to be telling you something about Mark at the same time. Skilfully used, it could indicate that Mark has paused to think ('carefully'); to give himself time to gather his thoughts. In a thriller, it might be preparing you for Mark's next move, which is to go for his gun.

Ideally, every word you write should count, should be earning its keep. This usually means, if you follow the rule, discarding whole chunks of writing you're particularly fond of or indeed proud of. Ask yourself: do they truly advance the storyline? Or are they adding to the reader's knowledge of the characters? If not, they are probably weakening, not strengthening your story and should end up in the wastepaper basket – with a few tears of bereavement.

Your slip is showing
'History is bunk,' said Henry Ford in the course of a libel suit in 1919, and one knows instinctively what he meant. There has been a strong current of opinion, especially in certain educational circles, that the same is true of grammar. If you can express yourself fluently in terms readily understood, why bother with semantics? Language, the argument runs, is a living thing, formed by colloquialism – its popular usage – not by some antiquated rules. It's arguable both ways, but I would say that whereas 'common usage' may be acceptable in everyday conversation and correspondence, even in normal business, it should not be acceptable in the written work of those whose business is the manipulation of the English language. If you are a craftsman by profession, you should be trained to use the proper tools; not because of some guild fetish but because they are the ones that serve you best. Makeshift tools won't do as good a job.

If you are a professional writer, it's not so much a question of showing off, or not showing your ignorance, as of conveying the precise sense of what you mean to say. English is a profoundly subtle language, and the slack use of it blurs where it should clarify. 'Disinterested', to take a random example from the list that follows, doesn't mean the same as 'uninterested', though it is commonly used as a synonym. If you use it like that, what do you write when you want to make the distinction between the two?

I referred, at the beginning of this book, to Fowler's *Modern English Usage* and make no apology for referring to it again, if only to say that I'm not about to attempt anything at quite the same lofty level. All I am about to do is to list some of the most common mistakes I have come across repeatedly in all the years I've been reading authors' MSS (plus a few personal hobby horses of my own), on the off-chance that though many of them will strike you as obvious – if not insulting – there just might creep in the occasional one you have been guilty of yourself. I base this on personal experience. As a writer, I have been guilty of silly mistakes all my life, and still am – until some kind person points them out.

In somewhat arbitrary but alphabetical order, then:

Alright
I know we have already and always, but 'all right' remains obstinately two separate words. It's no use pretending you're writing cockney dialogue, because the pronunciations are identical. Sadly it still appears in some printed books, and is spreading.

Apostrophes
Indicating the genitive, or possessive, case. If you leave them out carelessly you end up with phrases like 'babies rattle'. They don't.

Balmy (fragrant, soothing)
Often wrongly used for barmy (dotty).

Commas

The most frequently encountered and easily the worst mistake is to use them to make a sort of forced marriage between two quite unconnected sentences. 'Jacqueline came into the room, she went to the window . . .' has two subjects (*Jacqueline* and *she*) when it needs only one. Substitute 'Jacqueline came into the room and went to the window . . .' or 'Jacqueline came into the room, went to the window and looked out', or 'Jacqueline came into the room; she went to the window', or 'Jacqueline came into the room. She went to the window' – all of which are correct. The second common mistake is the misuse of commas to isolate a phrase in parenthesis; that is to say an 'aside' which could be removed from the main sentence without destroying the meaning. 'Jacqueline came into the room(,) timing her entrance perfectly, and went to the window'. The bracketed comma completes the pair you need to isolate the 'aside' and prevent it ruining the construction. Used in this way, commas stand for brackets. Can you imagine one bracket by itself?

The third common mistake is to leave them out in dialogue before the name of the person addressed: 'Do you know, John?' is not the same as 'Do you know John?' (Yes, I know John. We were at school together.)

Compare to, compare with

These are frequently muddled. *To* indicates a similarity; *with* a comparison. Vauxhall-Opel once launched a massive advertising campaign on television and in the press based on the slogan, 'Before you buy any car . . . compare it to a Vauxhall or Opel,' thus unwittingly inviting the obvious response, 'Oh yes, this new car I'm thinking of buying is just like a Vauxhall (or Opel).' To compare him *with* Tolstoy could mean the opposite (compared with Tolstoy, he is illiterate).

Deprecate, depreciate

The first expresses strong disapproval, deplores. The second diminishes in value, often used modestly about one's own achievements. 'Oh, it was nothing,' she said deprecatingly – can't be right.

Different from

Not to. But 'different than' is acceptable in American English.

Disinterested

This means impartial; it doesn't mean uninterested. The linesman at a tennis match is a disinterested spectator: he doesn't mind who wins. Which doesn't mean that he isn't interested in the match.

Due

If you begin a sentence 'Due to . . .' ninety-nine times out of a hundred you are wrong and should be ashamed of yourself, along with a million others. 'Due' in this sense is an adjective and must refer to a noun, not to an idea. 'His limp is due to a war wound' is correct. 'Due to a war wound he limps' is not. Use 'Owing to'.

Farther, further

Commonly treated as synonymous, which is a waste of a word. Correctly, farther (the comparative of far) refers to distance, and further to quality, as 'furthermore'. But the distinction has become blurred like much formal grammar through popular usage.

Floating participle

Perhaps the most common mistake of all and one that will probably pass unnoticed. Nevertheless you should be aware of it, if only because it could destroy your original sense. 'Climbing the hill between fine groves of olive trees, the house stood alone on the summit.' Either a road was climbing or somebody was, but as both possible subjects have disappeared, the only thing left to

climb is the house; a good, if simple example of a writer saying
what he never meant. To paraphrase a letter in *The Times* (from a
publisher!): 'Replying to Mrs X's letter the pig in question
was . . .' Well, whatever the pig was doing, it wasn't replying to
Mrs X's letter. If you start with an ' . . . ing' sort of word (the par-
ticiple, or verbal adjective), don't let go of the noun it was originally meant to describe. This can apply too, of course, to simple
adverbs, as with the popular and sloppy use of hopefully, which
means in a manner full of hope. Larry Adler on a radio pro-
gramme quoted a vivid example of the misuse of this word:
'Hopefully the prisoner will be executed tomorrow' (the speaker
hopes he will; the prisoner doesn't).

Forte
Italian, not French. But I've seen forté many times.

Hers, ours, theirs, yours
These are already possessive; no apostrophe please.

I – me
A possible hangover from playgroup days: 'Don't say "Me and
Peter", say "Peter and I".' Thus brainwashed, the child being
father to the man ends up writing 'First and second prizes were
presented to Peter and I.' Remove the words 'Peter and' and the
mistake positively glares at you. Nobody is capable of saying 'to I'
except in deeply rural districts. Examples like 'She couldn't
choose between Peter and I', 'Most of the runs were made by
Peter, who played brilliantly, and I' are only slightly less obviously
wrong.

If
'Much virtue in If,' Touchstone said. For the writer, it has as much
virtue as a landmine in his path. Probably another hangover from

early schooldays, when most of us at one time write 'If I was you' and had it severely corrected to 'If I were you'. Quite right too. But unhappily in many cases this led to the solid conviction that 'If I was' is invariably wrong, and that 'If' must invariably be followed by the subjunctive (conditional or hypothetical) tense of the following verb. Neither is true. Use the subjunctive only in hypothetical or impossible situations. 'If I were you' (I'm not); 'If I was mistaken' (perhaps I was), for instance, yesterday, which takes us into the past tense, which authors use most of the time and which can look complicated. Fowler runs to four pages on subjunctives, but for our immediate purposes I suggest a simple test. When you are stuck between 'She thought that if she were to marry Jonathan she would insist on a white wedding', and 'She thought that if she was to marry Jonathan . . .' all you have to do is to ask yourself what (in the present tense) the potential bride actually thinks. Does she think to herself 'If I am to marry . . .' that is, expecting to, in which case the simple past tense is *was*; or does she think 'If I were to marry . . .' that is, unreal, perhaps wishful thinking, in which case the hypothetical *were*, again subjunctive because it indicates no certainty.

Infer, imply

Two words frequently confused as if they were synonyms (a hypothetical subjunctive because they aren't; *pace* the *Concise Oxford Dictionary* which allows it). To infer is to deduce from something. To imply means to indicate obliquely, to hint at. You say, 'Well, of course!' implying that you knew that already. I infer that you did. If you accept the words as synonymous you are losing a subtlety. You read aloud from a newspaper article which says all writers are vain, and you look at me (a writer). I could say, 'Are you implying that I am vain?' (Is that what you are telling me in this oblique way?). Or I could say, 'Are you inferring that I am vain?' (Is that the meaning you are reading into the report itself?)

Its, it's
'Its' is possessive, meaning 'belonging to it'. 'It's' stands for 'It is'
as in 'It's my birthday' or 'It has' as in 'It's just occurred to
me.'

Lay, lie
The first is transitive, the second intransitive; that is, you have to
lay something (usually a table, or an egg if you are a hen); and you
can't lie anything. I suspect the confusion arises, when it does,
because of course lay is also the past tense of lie (whereas the past
tense of lay is laid.) No matter how often you hear 'Lay down' (in
popular songs for instance) it's always wrong. (But 'As I lay me
down to sleep' is fine). How often have you read 'She was laying on
the bed'?

Masterful, masterly
Easily confused because both mean 'having the manner of a master'. The first correctly refers to the perhaps overbearing master
over others (schoolmaster; authoritarian, bossy); the second to
the master of his art, by implication highly skilful. Of course it
applies to women too – 'the manner of a mistress' could be mis-
construed.

Mislaid possessives
'I hate you calling me Porky.' 'Do you mind me asking you?' 'She
loved Julian telling off the traffic warden.' I don't hate you; what I
hate is being called Porky. You don't mind me; she didn't love
Julian; she loved what he did. Read 'your', 'my', 'Julian's'.

None
Means 'not one'. 'None of the thirty-four shops in the high street
is (not are) open on Sundays.'

No one

Has to be two words to avoid the midday look of 'noone'. A hyphen, no-one, seems to be increasingly popular but still isn't correct.

Philistine

This is probably too deeply embedded in the language for any attempt to wrest it back to its original sense to have a chance of success. But, as a matter of interest, the compilers of the Old Testament didn't much care for the Philistines, who never survived to protest that they themselves were miles in advance of the Hebrews in art and technology and no doubt regarded the Hebrews as pretty uncouth at the time. To call a person a Philistine, as one unappreciative of culture, is to stand the word on its head. (The German universities started the rot with Philister for the 'town', the non-student; hence an outsider and thence an uneducated person, a prole or yob.)

Pristine

Likewise. Very much an 'in' word, and a very useful one in the sense of bandbox-new, fresh-as-a-daisy, like newly settled snow. The fact that it doesn't mean anything of the sort is probably of no great importance; eventually, no doubt, it will. If a boy tells his girlfriend her dress is pristine, she is unlikely to be aware that the primary meaning of the word is ancient. It is correctly applied to very, very old artefacts which have been preserved in more or less their original excellent, pristine condition. Considering their age, of course. A journalist writing in the *Daily Telegraph* magazine recently referred to 'factory-finished modern fabrics' as 'pristine'.

Scotch

Whisky – though never called Scotch in Scotland – or broth, the people being Scots or Scottish. (Actually not a grammatical mistake; but the Scots prefer it that way.)

Shall, will

Almost nobody gets this right, and if you can't be bothered you will be in good company; but there is a difference, and again you are losing shades of meaning if you blur it. Confusion arises because there are two quite different verbs which in everything except the first person ('I' and 'we') are spelled and pronounced in the same way; and both words are will. I called them verbs, but strictly speaking the first is an auxiliary verb. Attached to any regular verb it simply expresses the future tense, as 'She will go to university when she is eighteen'. A fact. The second comes from the proper verb to will, to be willing. 'She will keep teasing the cat.' Intention: she likes teasing the cat. It could just conceivably be a simple statement about the future, but the odds are against it. From even these two examples, you can see there's a lot of overlap; but since the two words come out the same it's not going to matter if you don't actually know which one you are using – except, as we just noted, in the first person. And that's where practically everybody comes a cropper. The verb 'to will' in the present tense never changes its form – don't write to me; I know it changes in the old 'thou willest', 'God willeth', but we're considering modern English – it remains plain 'will'. The auxiliary, however, does change from will to shall when it follows 'I' or 'we', and this is the bit to watch out for. 'I shall go to London tomorrow' is our friend the auxiliary merely helping the verb to go into the simple future: stating a fact (in so far as one can state facts about tomorrow). But 'I will go to London tomorrow', though also a statement about the future, is expressing intention: I will; I want; I intend. To quote an illustration from my own remote schooldays: a foreign gentleman had the misfortune to fall into an English river and cried for help in these words: 'I will be drowned, and no one shall save me!' Naturally, the erudite locals reasoned that if he wanted to be drowned they had best leave him to it.

If you have followed me so far, you should have no difficulty in grasping that the parallel, conditional forms follow the identical rule: 'I (or we) should be grateful . . .' is the neutral auxiliary again. 'I (or we) would go if I (we) could . . .' indicates intention or purpose, even if frustrated. You are now a better man or woman, Gunga Din, than most of those educated people who write every day to *The Times* letters beginning with the impossible (but admittedly very commonly accepted) construction 'I would like to say . . .' You will know that would here comes from the verb to will, not from the auxiliary, and you can't be willing to like something. The correct form is either 'I should like to say' or 'I would say' – which mean precisely the same thing. The same of course applies to all verbs expressing preference: 'I would prefer' can't be right.

Having (hopefully) cleared up this point, I hesitate to muddy the waters, but the perspicacious reader will have spotted an anomaly in the words of the drowning foreigner (no one shall save me); and I just wrote 'you should have no difficulty . . .'

This isn't something one needs to worry about because hardly anybody gets it wrong, but in fact it is a further and different use of shall and should which remains constant throughout (all three persons) and expresses determination, obligation or demand: or a sense of ought. 'I should go' (but I'm not going). 'They shall not pass.'

Titles
If you confer titles on fictional characters, check to make sure you've got them right. The most common mistake is with the ladies. Charmain, Lady Vibart, is the wife or widow of Lord Vibart or Sir John Vibart (before she married him she was plain Charmain Brown), a courtesy title which she loses if she remarries. Lady Charmain Vibart is a lady in her own right, daughter of an earl at least, perhaps married to a Mr Vibart. Or she could equally well be unmarried, Vibart being her maiden name. The first is referred to as Lady Vibart, the second as Lady Charmain. (This is

why the late Lord George-Brown wasn't able to be Lord George Brown, which would have made him Lord George, because it applies to men too.)

Try to
Not try and. You can of course try and try again, but you can't try and see. You aren't trying and seeing, you are trying to see.

Whisky, whiskey
The former for Scottish and Canadian; American and Irish kinds are spelt with the 'e'.

Who(m)
'The man whom I saw going into the shop' is correct. 'The woman whom I thought loved me was unfaithful' is not. In the first example we have in essence 'I saw the man'; in the second the impossible 'I thought the woman' instead of 'who (I thought) loved me'. Sadly the proper use of the word whom is almost disappearing from the language these days. Hilarious quote from a *Daily Telegraph* article on women in business: 'many men derive . . . pleasure from encouraging clever young women whom they feel [*sic*] deserve their help'.

Wilful
This, like 'skilful', drops the first 'l' (of 'will' and 'skill') as well as the expected second one, which all the '-full' endings drop. Obvious, but many MSS are presented with 'hopefulls' and 'wishfulls', so if this is your slip you are not alone. 'Skillful' and 'willful' are acceptable in US English, however.

Wrack
A perfectly good, if rare, English noun meaning seaweed or wreckage washed up on the shore. Rack, without the 'w', is the well-

known instrument of torture, and the application of it, from which we derive the near-literal 'racked with pain' and the metaphorical 'to rack one's brains'.

First person singular

Unless you are writing a formula romantic novel, in which case the commissioning editor might object to it, there's no reason why you shouldn't present your fiction in the form of a first-person narrative, if that's what you want to do.

It looks easier, and to some extent it is: you identify yourself strongly with your narrator; never have to avoid the trap of the 'invisible author' because the author – in the sense of the 'I' who is telling the story – in this case is meant to be visible. He (or she) is the only one you have to worry about in terms of internal dialogue; everybody else and every scene and setting is straightforwardly described through his or her eyes. This makes for good continuity and saves no end of trouble. But there are snags.

You have limited yourself to telling your reader only what the narrator knows. Out goes the useful device of 'Meanwhile, back at the ranch . . .' There is also the problem of making the narrator an attractive or at least sympathetic (in the literary sense of allowing for reader-identification) character, which has to be put across somewhat obliquely. One way of tackling this is by a sort of feedback. You can't have your pretty girl admiring herself in the looking glass and escape the charge of conceit; someone else has to say it (in her hearing; even to her. She – the 'I' – takes this as outrageous flattery, but you convey to the reader that it's true. This makes her pretty and modest).

The narrator needs to be identified quickly, even more quickly than a conventional third-person character. I once found in a library the very first novel by a now famous female novelist. As I didn't recognize the title, and the publisher wasn't the novelist's usual one, I was intrigued enough to take it home and read it. It opened with the narrator standing on a bridge and, as I recall, about to jump off, only to be rescued by a nice man with an invitation back to his flat. There followed pages of dialogue and so on, until the narrator went to bed in the spare room. The next morning, on about page six, the narrator got up, went into the bathroom and shaved. (That was difficult to write without mentioning 'he': of course, knowing the author, I had assumed it was a 'she' all along.)

I said the first-person approach was to some extent easier, limited to what the narrator knows, but in its finest forms it can call for unusual skills not to be dismissed as easy at all: far from it. A superb example of the way in which this can be handled is Keith Waterhouse's first (and sadly unacclaimed) novel, *There Is a Happy Land*, in which he tells the story in the first person through the eyes of a young schoolboy. The really clever bit is that the narrator is describing events which he doesn't fully understand but in such a way that the reader does.

At this level the first person narrative can be far more of a challenge than the more usual story-telling.

Dialogue

Competent writers of non-fiction not infrequently run into difficulties when attempting a novel, and one of the major difficulties is handling dialogue: where you are writing something not unlike a playscript, quoting the speaker's actual words but with the added complication that you have to work them into your narrative so that the reader knows exactly who says what without the speakers' presence, as in a radio play.

As in a playscript, you should normally allow a fresh paragraph for each change of speaker. That's the rule. You can break it, and writers do, but you ought to have good reason for doing so. Otherwise it's a useful device for keeping your reader abreast.

The common device for indicating who is speaking, as we all

know, is to write the spoken words in quotes with the key words *Jack said, said Jill, he said* or *she said*. You can go on using 'said' until the cows come home and nobody will object or even notice. It is a small inconspicuous word that draws little attention to itself. Don't strain to avoid repetition by introducing exotic variations like 'ejaculated he' or 'she remonstrated'. Substitutes for 'said' which don't describe the act of speaking, like 'she pouted', 'he sniffed' should be used with discretion or they look awful. (But 'he laughed' is fine.) Of course there are many perfectly good substitutes for 'said' – whispered, cried, shouted and so on, but they should be used with discretion and in their proper places. When all the speaker does is to say something in a normal voice, stick to 'said'.

Admittedly, the endless use of 'said' can become tedious to you, if not to the reader. The best way to avoid its over-use is to avoid it altogether. In extended dialogue you can often leave it out, if who is speaking is obvious anyway. Provided it is.

A boy meets a girl.

'Hallo,' she said.

'Hallo.'

(It's pretty clear, even to the dimmest reader, that she isn't speaking to herself. You can carry on like this.)

'How are you?'

'I'm fine. How's your mother?'

'Great. How's your father?'

'Same as usual. I say –'

'Yes?'

'I've got something for you.'

'And I've got something for you.'

'Shake.'

If you read that quickly and can swear with your hand on your heart who said 'Shake', you're doing well. Somewhere along the line, the thing's gone off the rails. Mainly because the actual spoken words offer no clue. If she had said, 'Hey! You've grown a moustache', or he'd said, 'I do believe you're pregnant', there would have been no problem. Failing that, we need a little help. If you want to avoid 'he/she said' try adding the odd, independent sentence to bring the speaker into focus. Thus:

'Same as usual. I say –'

'Yes?' Jill took his arm.

'I've got something for you.'

Or you could reverse the order:

Jill took his arm. 'Yes?'

Note that in each case the character's action comes on the same line as the words spoken, indicating that they belong together. Either way, we are back on firm ground. If you're writing well this will also be telling you something about Jill: that her feelings are friendly. I mentioned just now the misuse of words not descriptive of the act of speaking, which shouldn't lightly or carelessly be offered as substitutes for words that do. I read a popular novel with innumerable examples, of which I quote just one at random.

'You should know. Never mind', she brushed away his apologies.

Well, I suppose if you wrote 'never mind' on a blackboard you could brush it away; but you can see what's happened. A full stop after 'mind' and a capital 's' for 'She' would have made it perfectly correct usage. (What was the publisher's editor doing to pass it?)

The quotes used for dialogue may be double (" ") or single (' '). It doesn't matter which, but see House Style on page 179. Unspoken thoughts, which themselves are a form of (inner) dialogue, may be in quotes but are probably better off without, to avoid confusion.

If you tape the words of almost any normal, everyday conversation, then transfer them to typescript, you will find them unreadable. Few of us speak fluently off the cuff, avoid repetition or hole-plugging 'um's' and 'er's' or express our thoughts in concise sequence extempore. Consequently, the novelist has to cheat all the time. This can be overdone by making your characters continuously utter beautifully turned phrases when it would be quite out of character. You can hint at some incoherence by staggering the dialogue a bit – but not too much. Everything your characters say should be relevant to the storyline and theme or to the individual character of the speaker, while at the same time looking or sounding natural. If in doubt, try reading your dialogue aloud. Most conversations contain a good deal of dross that is neither relevant nor important. These are the parts that should be ruthlessly excised from your book. If you are writing really well, the speakers' manner of speech and idiosyncratic phrases will identify them, as in a script for radio.

3 Singletons or occasional writing

We shall be looking presently at the function of literary agents, to whom a majority of new authors at least think of turning for guidance through the publishing jungle; and the reason I mention them here is because if you are starting out by trying your hand at articles, short stories or poems, you are probably on your own. Agents will normally handle occasional, short pieces of prose or poetry only as a service for regular clients, which usually means book authors, because the commission they could expect to earn bears no relation to the work involved. (Some who do handle occasional pieces will charge a very much inflated commission.) In any case, the help an agent can give at this stage will be very limited, it being uphill work to persuade a magazine or journal to pay more than 'standard' rates for a newcomer.

Prose

It is not impossible to write, say, a short story with no particular market in mind and thereafter to find a magazine or journal whose editor finds it exactly right in content, style and length; but it isn't too likely. It is even less likely with an article.

I said earlier that you should consider the market before you begin writing. With articles this is self-evident: only an idiot would submit something on yachting to *Horse & Hound*, and even with less specialized subjects it isn't difficult to work out where the interest lies. With short stories it's less obvious, but the principle is the same. If you are writing for a magazine, it's only common sense to read the magazine first – preferably a number of issues – to attune yourself to the sort of readership it's aimed at, the length and style preferred. Magazines have certain types, classes or categories which make up the majority of their readership, and it's the editor's job to provide the sort of stuff they like reading. It's your job too.

The Writers' and Artists' Yearbook (this year's one, not an old one you've found in the attic) will give you a sound indication of the journal's requirements and the length of contributions they will consider and sometimes the rate of payment. It's a good and useful start but no substitute for closer study.

Submit your article, professionally set out, to the appropriate editor – this might be the features editor or fiction editor, for example. If they like it, they will offer their standard fee, calculated on the number of words, which, as we've noted, an agent will be unlikely to improve on for an unknown writer, though he might do very much better for an established author. You may get a rejection slip, since editors get an awful lot of MSS and can't be expected to write individual letters for each one they turn down. If you're lucky, though, you may get a letter of criticism, indicating that the editor liked your work, which wasn't quite right for them, and would like to see more from you. In which case, try again; keep in touch and tailor your next in the way suggested until, God willing, you get on the same wavelength and become a regular contributor. Sometimes an occasional piece complies with the known requirements of more than one journal, in which case you will certainly try them all.

With articles especially, the fee will be modest sometimes so modest – in particular with highbrow journals with modest circulations – virtually the only reward will be seeing your name in print. But it's still excellent practice and, who knows, it may well lead on to better things.

With short stories, a correspondence school may be helpful. I don't myself think they can teach you talent, but they can teach you how to plan and plot and where to look for ideas (news items can be a trigger). I dare say many writers, like myself, began by reading magazine stories and thinking, any fool can write this; only to discover that this particular fool couldn't. Even the slightest of romantic stories published is written without – well, let's say *almost* without – exception by a professional who knows exactly what he or she (probably she) is doing. If at first you don't succeed, try to grasp why. It may be that your tongue was too firmly embedded in your cheek; in which case try another angle. I discovered quite soon that I could manage this by a deliberately light, humorous approach, after which I sold stories quite regularly in a market I'd previously failed to break into.

With the exception of humorous articles, which depend on the writer's style and perhaps an idiosyncratic view of commonplace material, the author of an article writes from a peculiar knowledge of his subject or at least an original approach to it. The message is the thing; all else is simply the professional presentation, which usually means clarity. Wit and elegance is a plus, but the facts are what count.

Fiction is a bit different. The short story is, essentially, a miniature novel – though some, like Dorothy Parker's, can be little gems, perfect in themselves. Indeed professional writers of fiction have been known to spurn the short story on the grounds that any really good plot can usually be extended to make a full-length novel. There is a lot of truth in this; but personally I would recommend the short story as an excellent training ground for novelists, if only because it forces the writer to accept the discipline of paring down, a skill which could stand the writer in good stead later. If your short story can't be reduced to the maximum number of words your particular market will stand, you should forget it. I would say that if you can express yourself in something like half the words you would have liked to use, you are well on the way to becoming professional. And of course the essential layout is the same in all fiction.

There are very roughly three markets for the short story, all, alas, limited these days except for well-known authors. The first, most obvious and most remunerative, is the popular, mass-market magazine. This will reach thousands and thousands of readers, payment will be good and competition quite fierce. The second is the 'literary' magazine, with a modest circulation, which will pay badly but may catch the eye of publishers or agents and lead to better things. The third is the occasional volume of new writers put out from time to time by book publishers to capture new authors on the grounds of literary merit, or volumes which will accommodate new as well as established authors if their stories fit comfortably into the categories wanted for a collection (crime, horror, ghost, etc.). Watch out for these (and see also Collected Stories on page 87).

Verse

Apart from the Poet Laureate, poets form the one exception to the rule that one should write for a more or less specific market. Poets write to please themselves, and so they should. On the other hand, they can rarely expect more than a derisory remuneration, and writing verse is no way of making a living; if there are more than a thimbleful who do, I'd be surprised. To become established or recognized as a poet, you need to have at least one book of verse published. Few publishers expect to make money out of publishing poetry, since very few people buy books of verse other than the classics, but some publishers will publish all the same if they consider it outstanding. Nevertheless, the chances for a book of poetry by an unknown poet are slim.

The best approach is to submit individual poems to the various journals and magazines which publish occasional verses. If you can get a fair number published in this way, individually, then is the time to collect them together – probably with additional poems – for offer to a book publisher. Acknowledgements should be made to the journals that first printed them, but provided you've previously granted only limited, once-off rights, no formal permission is required. Their previous publication will influence the book publisher and may well tilt the scales in your favour.

Agents are unenthusiastic about handling poetry for the simple reason that they involve a great deal of work for a very small remuneration; but they do handle them all the same. Popular poets are constantly approached for permission to quote their verse in anthologies, for which a fee must be negotiated and copyright cleared. Often the fee is as little as a few pounds, but as collectively these make up the poet's income, something is usually insisted on.

4 Books

The object of writing a book is to get it published at somebody else's expense (see Vanity Publishing on page 134); and the object of publishing a book is to sell as many copies as possible. Hardback – also called hardcover or clothbound – books were purchased by libraries (which increasingly take paperback books if they can afford to take books at all!), institutions, bookclubs, as gifts, and occasionally by people who actually want to read them when they come out, instead of waiting hopefully for the cheaper paperback edition. Libraries especially work on an ever-shrinking budget and, whereas certain categories of books used to rely heavily, if not entirely, on this market, it is no longer the case. Hence the near-demise of light romantic fiction in hardcover, such being widely borrowed rather than bought. Even with the welcome arrival of the Public Lending Right, the return to the author is meagre compared with regular royalties on sales. Nothing is calculated to irritate an author more than the flattering remark 'I did enjoy your book,' followed by 'I got it out of the library.'

You may have noticed that there exists an ingrained resistance to buying books, primarily among people who tell you they can't afford them. You recall their satellite dish, video tapes, computer games – perhaps their habit of eating out when a halfway decent meal costs more than the average book – and boggle. I don't myself believe the excuse that books are expensive is valid, because in cost-of-living terms they aren't. The author, looking at his royalty statement, may well think them dirt cheap. Nevertheless, they are (unless directly *useful*, see Books-as-tools on page 65) commonly thought of as an extravagance, and I believe the reason is that we have long been accustomed to having them available for nothing from public libraries. The fact that some libraries will no longer order copies of fiction on request may eventually change this, but it will take time.

That having been said, it would be ungracious not to acknowledge that libraries, like bookclubs which also horribly reduce the return to the author, do represent a welcome and useful outlet in so far as they make some books available to people who otherwise would go without rather than buy them.

Of course some hardback books, like some pop records, do sell in quite enormous numbers, if often at heavily reduced rates. The fact that the percentage of those published or issued is minute should not deter us from aiming at the legitimate trade market, which remains the prime one. And the way to it is through a narrow door marked 'Publisher's Editor'.

The author sees his book as a magnificent creation which a great many people will enjoy reading. The editors may agree – they may not – with a slight variation: a book a great many people would enjoy reading. If, that is, they ever got to hear of it and if they could be persuaded to buy – or even borrow – it. Which is, sad to say, not a good and sufficient reason for publishing it. This is the hurdle at which so many fall. Unless the editors can see a way of clearing the hurdle, they will in all likelihood decline to make an offer. The trouble is, there are rather a lot of books published in the UK each week (6,000–7,000 would be a fair guess, including reprints), and booksellers can't possibly stock more than a tiny fraction. Fewer still get to the front of the crowd clamouring for review space.

An incalculable number of books an equally incalculable number of people would enjoy reading never see the light of day or, if published at all, see at best a watery dawn.

The hurdle may be overcome by 'the hype', by luck or even by merit. By the hype if the publisher for one of several reasons reckons that the book will respond to heavy publicity coupled with a very substantial first printing. Nothing in publishing succeeds like success, and the trade will generally respond to the news that 100,000 copies are in the press, the author has been paid a six-figure advance and the publisher (no fool) has in effect put his shirt on it. But the investment is hair-raising and clearly involves sums not available every day; nor could the publisher thus channel his finances into more than a very few of the books on his list. This gamble doesn't always work, but may with luck. Luck is something we all need; occasionally it works almost without prompting, when a book which has had the benefit of precious little promotion, or virtually none, and few if any reviews, catches on by word of mouth and becomes a bestseller almost despite this apparent neglect. (I have known this happen more than once but won't embarrass anyone by quoting titles.) As for merit, it's something not to be discounted in all but a few bestsellers; but merit is closely associated with luck. Some, such as *Captain Corelli's Mandolin*, after a modest start, over the next couple of years built up to bestsellerdom.

Books sell on the author's name, on the subject or on a combination of the two. In that order. This places the new writer in a don't-go-into-the-water-until-you-can-swim situation. The only consolation is that, with the exception of celebrities and the occasional hype, every author started like this.

A film used to be a tremendous boost for the sales of the book on which it was based. Nowadays it is television which, of course, reaches a fantastically increased audience. But in both cases, with the number of properties up for sale, it's very much a buyer's market. By the time a film is screened or staged the book could well be out of print; examples of this are *Aspects of Love* and *Jurassic Park*. Amazingly, neither of these novels was available anywhere when either film was released. But the author does get a share of the film's profits.

Non-fiction

The term non-fiction covers a multitude of syndromes: virtually every type of book there is except novels, collections of stories and verse. It is impossible to postulate any kind of formula covering the field. But it may be worth considering some of the more common areas of non-fiction.

We touched on celebrity books earlier. Somewhat illogically it's assumed that popular success in one field is a qualification for pontificating on all manner of subjects which have nothing to do with it and tends to ensure a wide readership because people recognize the name. That isn't to say that celebrities are necessarily ignorant of these matters – no reason why a film star shouldn't be expert on aerobics (or make a good president) – but with books it does give them a flying start, and it makes sense to exploit the advantage. Until you become a celebrity yourself, grin and bear it. Which is the last word on celebrities. Let's look at the more conventional categories of non-fiction books attempted by the rest of us.

One major advantage in tackling non-fiction is that there is often no need to write a whole book to find out if it's viable. A high proportion of published non-fiction works has been commissioned by the publishers on the strength of a synopsis and a specimen chapter or two (see Synopses and Specimen Material on page 103). A possible disadvantage is that someone else might bring out a book on the same subject just before you've finished yours. There's no foolproof way of avoiding this risk. Attempts have been made to set up a register of titles and subjects, but it's never worked and is probably unworkable anyway. However, if you are researching your subject as you go along, you may well discover if someone else is fishing in the same waters and be alerted. A similar book published simultaneously with yours may, contrariwise, turn out to be no bad thing. Such books are often complementary and get reviewed together, which gives them a better chance of review space.

It need hardly be said – but I'll say it – that it's vital to get your facts right and to quote your sources for controversial material. Non-fiction books, unlike novels, are sent out for review by experts in the particular field, who are only too ready to seize upon factual errors if only to prove that they *are* experts.

Autobiography
The popular and very natural choice of the older man or woman with an urge to write, retired or perhaps these days redundant, or when the kids have grown up and left home. They have always wanted to write something, now have the leisure and, dammit, they've had a jolly interesting Life which would make a good book.

It probably wouldn't.

Another favourite half-truth is that everyone has a book in them. True, a lot of people have had interesting lives; in a sense almost everybody's life story could be made interesting if presented brilliantly enough, but sadly not everybody is that brilliant, and anyway no one is going to know how brilliant until they open the book. And the autobiography of someone whose name on the jacket means absolutely nothing to the reading public is a complete outsider unless the publisher can announce why the life will be of great interest. (The psychic who foretold Maxwell's death and found Lord Lucan?)

However, if you are determined, take a chance by all means and prove me wrong – all the best books prove somebody wrong. But if you can, stick to one central theme. It may be childhood memories of village life in Yorkshire or Brazil, running a pub, living as a tramp or being awarded the VC. (I've handled successful autobiographies on all these themes.) But if you happened to have experienced all four, the narrative will end up disjointed, with your own personality the only connecting link, and unless you can make yourself personally interesting, as against relying on your experiences, you're unlikely to hit the jackpot.

Perhaps you can. You should certainly try. Don't leave yourself out on the grounds of modesty. You want the reader to share your experiences – which you obviously think worth sharing – to take a vicarious pleasure in them, to be amazed or scared stiff. Descriptions are for travel brochures. The fact that Mount Everest was climbed is in itself of limited interest today to anyone except a fellow mountaineer. What your average armchair reader wants to know is what it feels like to climb Everest. He wants to experience it, not be fed with statistics. This he can do only by identifying with the central character: you. So you must be a 'character' in your book. Also, bring in your companions, draw verbal pictures of them: your wife/husband, your family, if appropriate. Unless the readers are interested in them, they are unlikely to be terribly interested in the story.

Of course, this involves risks. Of sounding pompous or self-congratulatory. The reader will warm more readily to you if you recount the occasional mistake, when you made an ass of yourself, as well as when you won all those beauty competitions. It's a nice distinction, a fine line to tread, between over-modesty and arrogance. However, if you are determined to bare your soul, you have to risk it.

If you have a terrific story but can't get it together, you could use the services of an experienced writer to put it into shape for you (see Ghosts – Literary on page 89). But unless you are on to a certainty, with a publisher already lined up, and you can share the profits, it will be expensive because the 'ghost' will be looking to you, rather than to the publisher, for his pay cheque.

Biography
With a historical biography, the new writer is faced with an imme-

diate problem. If the subject is one likely to appeal to a wide public, because itself a familiar name in history, it is bound to have
been tackled before; probably several and perhaps many times.
However, if it hasn't been written about for some years and if you
have unearthed unpublished material or have a startling new
theory which you think you can substantiate, go ahead. Again,
bear in mind that it will be reviewed (if at all) by a respected
expert in this period or area, and experts have a tendency to take
unkindly to non-experts trumping their aces and will therefore
pick all the holes that are to be picked. If you have a formidable
string of letters after your name you will be treated with more
respect, but your reviewer may well have an even longer string,
and his views may clash violently with yours – and there's every
chance that he'll be an old colleague.

So you turn to someone who hasn't been written about; or not
much. This could give you a clear field. But, however fascinating
the life may be, the subject is unlikely to ring many bells with your
browser-in-bookshops, and as your name won't either how is the
poor publisher going to launch you?

None of this will deter you if you are convinced that you have
something original and interesting to say; nor should it. Others
have overcome these obstacles, so why not you?

Your first step will be to obtain every available publication on
or relevant to your subject, to add to your knowledge, to check
that your particular approach hasn't been made before and finally
that nothing closely resembling it has come out recently. It's
worth saying again: get your facts right. Even a few errors of prov-
able facts will tend to discredit an otherwise sound work.

With contemporary biography, your subject need not be living,
and indeed deceased subjects offer the somewhat unfair advantage to the biographer that he can say what he likes about them
without falling foul of the libel law (see Libel on page 163), unfortunately a loophole much to the advantage of popular biogra-

phers of the deceased by introducing often poorly substantiated skeletons in the cupboard – the 'feet of clay' syndrome – to diminish reputations of the famous for popular appeal. But whether your subject be alive or dead, your biography will be either authorized, or unauthorized (unauthorized biographies are not called unauthorized – unless the author makes a feature of the fact – but it will be obvious to the reader). For an authorized biography you will need to approach the subject if living, the family or executors of the estate if dead. The clear advantage is that you should be given access to papers, diaries, letters and anything else in the way of research material – in the case of the living, by the subject himself – which will be denied to others. You have a scoop.

The disadvantage is that the subject or estate will very likely want to approve what you have written and disallow anything they don't like, which could result in a whitewash; and they may expect a percentage of the profits. If the subject is a living celebrity, the percentage won't be less than half and could be more. Unless the celebrity is generously inclined – he will almost certainly have an agent or manager who won't be – or is a friend, he will also want the best and most sympathetic writer around and is unlikely to choose anyone who hasn't a proven record (see Ghosts – Literary on page 89).

Either way, it would be wise to ascertain whether a publisher is interested in principle. I have before now lined up a celebrity – which cost me an expensive though very enjoyable lunch – only to find that the publisher who originally wanted the book had changed his mind.

Bee-in-the-bonnet: polemics

You feel strongly, even passionately, about your subject, have a great deal to say of importance and a burning desire to communicate. Splendid. Line up the big guns of your argument and let fly. If what you have in mind is controversial, as it's almost bound to be, you will be galloping roughshod over the opinions of others stupid or misinformed enough to disagree with you. Did I hear you say, 'Serve them right'? Hang on a minute.

I remember a cartoon depicting two men at the end of a television interview. One, the big, bullying chap, is sitting back with a look of smug satisfaction. The other looks smaller and browbeaten, and he is saying meekly, 'I see now that the opinions I've held all these years have been quite wrong.'

The joke hardly needs explaining.

As the author, you hold the floor. The reader can't answer back. And this offers the temptation to tilt at windmills, to present his imagined objection in a form most easily demolished (not that Don Quixote's windmills were easy to demolish; but they presented no danger to the attacker), probably to ridicule them. This is more likely to offend than convert, which is presumably not your objective. Ridicule is risky because it provokes antipathy – the last thing the author wants; but it is fair game provided it is aimed at the opinions, not the person holding them (which he doesn't have to admit, after all), and provided it allows full and fair weight to the real objections held by many otherwise intelligent people and demolishes them by sheer logic. Preferably gently, letting them sink under their own weight: *reductio ad absurdam* may be the best way of achieving this.

A common ploy is the time-worn gambit: No intelligent person today believes . . . It saves a lot of time and effort, but it is an insult, not an argument. If, as is usually the case, a goodly number of intelligent people do believe the opposite of your claim, it is unlikely to convince any but the unthinking or those who already agree with you. It's the emperor's new clothes all over again.

It is fair enough to say that no intelligent person today believes that the earth is flat. It is manifestly untrue to say that no intelligent person today believes, say, in God, when there are at least as many intelligent theists as atheists. Such an assertion will antagonize the one and be pointless for the other, thus achieving less than nothing.

I said that the reader can't answer back. But don't forget that the book reviewer can and will, and he can repay you in your own coin: ridicule.

Travel

Like autobiography, travel is one of those subjects you probably shouldn't be writing about. You and your wife/husband/significant other being adventurous types, sold everything, including the house, equipped an elaborate Land-Rover, crossed half the globe and had lots of exciting adventures, which will make an exciting book – which you hope will recoup all the expenses.

Doubtful in the extreme. It's been done – and written about – before. At least two-thirds of the places you visited will be on the tourist routes – you can't avoid them all – and familiar to an awful lot of people, now foreign travel has become commonplace. And unless you write brilliantly and tremendously entertainingly – in which case a book on almost any subject has a sporting chance – your book is unlikely to have the sort of popular appeal which will persuade a publisher to take it on. In other words, the mere fact of having travelled widely won't carry the book.

True, if you've been somewhere where virtually nobody has been before the prospect will look brighter; but it's unlikely. (Marlo Morgan's story of her walkabout with Australian Aboriginals, *Mutant Message Down Under*, is a brilliant example of this.) If you're determined to write of your travels, and to finance them with a book and perhaps a newspaper serial, your best bet will be to have a theme. Just travelling for the hell of it won't do. A linking theme might change the picture. Suppose you visit exotic places to research, say, attitudes to feminism or to empire (in ex-colonial areas), wildlife and conservation, national cuisine or whatever else appeals to you. Invent a purpose for your travelling and you may be halfway there, because a purpose presupposes an answer in the end and rounds the book off. You don't even need an answer, come to that. I once handled a book by an adventurous woman who went in search of gorillas; the fact that she never actually found any didn't prevent the book from achieving publication. All the interesting and exciting travel bits were there, but the book was about gorillas – it could have been the Yeti – and that's why people picked it up and bought it.

I should warn you, however, that even if you have a smashing theme you will be unusually lucky if you get a publisher or newspaper to put up cash to help finance your travels. It's not impossible, but you have to see it from their side. Supposing you catch pneumonia at Dover or succumb to a poisoned arrow in the jungle . . .

As with mountaineering, remember to make your story personal: how it affected you yourself as a character and others with you. In a word, subjective. Otherwise you are writing a guidebook.

Guidebooks, which also come under this heading, present problems of a different sort. If you are uniquely qualified to write about a certain bit of the globe, and write well or at least lucidly, you may produce a good and useful book. Fine. However, it is unlikely to appeal to a publisher who doesn't go in for guidebooks; and publishers who do will very likely already have one on the same area. Before you begin, make sure that there's a real gap in this market. There may be.

Books-as-tools
You are reading one. I am writing it from an uncommon, working knowledge of the subject, because I know of nothing quite like it in print and because I believe (rightly or wrongly) that a lot of people will find it useful and will buy it – or rather vice versa. All this is comparatively straightforward because it falls in the simplest category of non-fiction: practical books designed primarily

to convey information rather than to entertain. (Naturally, if they entertain as well, so much the better.) This is the exception to the rule that books can be called an extravagance. They can't be if you are going to use them rather than read them once for fun; think of schoolbooks.

A dictionary is a prime example, but there are innumerable others from books on cookery, health, car maintenance to academic textbooks and books on diseases in sheep. Books, in fact, used as tools.

Assuming you already know something of what you're going to write about, this type of book presents fewer problems than most, but it isn't immune to the hazards of all non-fiction as we've noted: it will very likely be read and criticized by experts who know as much or more about the subject than you do. (So why didn't they write the book? Perhaps they didn't think of it, didn't have time, didn't want to or couldn't.) It behoves you to be accurate and, again, this involves research. Someone truthfully said that the best way to learn a subject is to write a book about it. Not only will it collect your thoughts into an organized form; it will also turn up facts you didn't previously know. Accuracy is the first essential. This is obvious enough in books on cookery or chemistry – you don't want to poison or blow up your readers – but applies to all.

I said the aim is to convey information rather than to entertain, and most schoolchildren will agree with me, but then they represent a captive audience. So in a sense do readers already interested in your subject and eager to read anything about it, however awful. But the book that entertains as well is bound to romp home leagues ahead of its rivals of the ditchwater sort. As with practically all books – *pace* lawyers and civil servants – the first desperate need is for lucid, unambiguous writing that's not in itself difficult to follow, even it the subject matter requires concentration. I have frequently enough come across examples which I could quote (but won't) where the true expert's book has fared far worse than a parallel book by a merely competent all-rounder, because the second was entertaining reading and the first anything but. This is partly due to the writer's skill (or want of it, see Style on page 29), but sometimes, too, due to the true expert's knowing *too* much, and being constitutionally unable to leave anything out. You will always end up knowing a lot more than will go into your book. The cookery writer is aware that if you put the mushrooms into a mushroom omelette too soon the omelette comes out grey; but most readers who are following the recipe properly would find this an unwelcome distraction. (Of course funny cookbooks do exist, like the bachelor's cookbook which recommends a 'heaped teaspoonful of dry sherry' but they wander out of this category.)

Incidentally, I threw in that 'merely' in mentioning the all-rounder only to emphasize the contrast; it wasn't meant to be derogatory. The implication is that the 'merely' competent chap who knows his stuff will be accurate enough but may produce little or no original material; rather a gathering together of known or published facts and others' opinions – sometimes rudely called a rehash – in a highly entertaining way not available in one volume elsewhere perhaps. This is not an adverse criticism. Every writer of non-fiction (almost) draws on the opinions of others in some form of rewriting and reassessment and would be unusual or foolish if he didn't.

The book-as-tool may originate with the publisher, who produces the idea and approaches a suitably qualified author if he knows one, or a literary agent if he doesn't. (The advantage of dealing through an agent is that if the author proves unsuitable it's the agent, not the publisher, who is going to be embarrassed.) Unless the author is a known and tried authority and has been published before, he will be asked to produce a sample of the work, in addition to a synopsis, before the publisher commits himself. If this involves more than a very nominal amount of work, a fee should be negotiated, which applies to a detailed synopsis which could be a scenario for an ambitious project; and a 'shut-off' fee if the whole thing falls through.

Most professional authors of books-as-tools stick to their last. They are necessarily specialists, and most specialist subjects provide scope for more than one book: probably several and possibly a whole series. Cookery again is one obvious example, but this applies equally well to many other broad subjects such as gardening, collecting antiques or, perhaps not surprisingly, sex. A dozen authors spring to mind whose name on the book is a hallmark of excellence or at least popularity. The more you write about your chosen subject, of course, the easier it gets, because the research accumulates until further research is hardly necessary. You are now one of the acknowledged experts, and you will be asked to review others' books and be thoroughly nasty about them.

Educational

We have already touched on education books in Books-as-tools, but perhaps they deserve a mention on their own, because they are to some extent *sui generis*, to the extent that, reversing the usual order, the demand comes first and the book is written to meet it. Hence they are almost invariably commissioned.

Publishers of educational books are usually specialists. They will be in close touch with their market and will be on the lookout for subjects, or aspects of subjects, where there is a gap; and they will look for a suitably qualified author to fill it. That author will be someone already known to them for his or her academic qualifications.

If nobody has actually asked you to write an educational book, if you know your stuff and your market – probably being in the business of education yourself, and aware of what books are available – and you have a Good Idea, then put together an outline and approach one of the educational publishers, stating clearly why you believe it is needed, will be popular and will sell like hot cakes.

The return, in terms of royalties, will be a lot less than you could expect from normal 'trade' books. On the other hand, there are two notable advantages: if your book is adopted by an educational authority it will be bound to sell in considerable numbers, since the purchasers have no option but to buy it; and there is a strong possibility that it won't 'date' as quickly as trade books do. Every new generation of schoolchildren or undergraduates will create a fresh demand.

Books for children
Non-fiction

Except for those aimed at the very young, books in this group are often written by authors who also write for adults, and it's easy to see why: the expertise in the subject is fundamentally the same; you've got to know your stuff. Adult books are sometimes reissued in 'junior' or 'cadet' editions, where the text is simplified and shortened, but the factual content remains essentially unchanged. There are few facets of professional writing that don't involve hard work, and this isn't one of them. To simplify – to make simple – calls for especial skills seldom apparent in the result (a point we shall return to), particularly when what you are trying to get across isn't simple at all. And 'simple' itself is a relative term. It doesn't mean moronic. I once struggled with a simple *Child's Guide to How Television Works* and never got beyond the first half-dozen pages, let alone the cat's-cradle diagrams. But the author knew his technically minded young readers.

Do I contradict myself? Very well – with apologies to Walt Whitman – I contradict myself. Here goes.

If you are fortunate enough to have this particular skill, or work hard enough to acquire it, it can open up a market for presenting common or garden general knowledge – which wouldn't make much of an adult book – in a way that makes it appeal to the young reader. You are still simplifying adult work, only in this case it isn't your own. Anne Terry White's adaptation of Rachel Carson's *The Sea Around Us* is a good example. Books of this sort are more often than not commissioned by a publisher to plug a gap in his list or in the market, in which case it will need to be 'tailored' to preconceived specifications as to length and vocabulary, perhaps to fit into a series, or for the educational market. This applies equally to –

Fiction
– if you are retelling the legends of King Arthur or Robin Hood or any classic tales in your own words.

Original story books or children's novels call for some additional skills, not only in the disciplined limitations of vocabulary and length but also in maintaining the pace of the narrative, which must never allow the attention to flag. On the whole children are not prepared to put as much effort into reading as (some) adults and they quickly become bored or distracted when not a lot is happening. You will have come across certain grown-up novels where the 'plot' is secondary, occasionally to the point of non-existence; for children it is of paramount importance. That's the first rule.

For 'plot' you can if you like read 'conflict'. All stories, when you think about it, are about conflict. If you haven't thought about it before, do so now: no conflict to overcome equals no story.

The second rule is that your young heroes and heroines must be active participants in the action: what they think, say and, especially, do should play a vital part in directing the development of the story. Don't make the mistake of having them, like the heroines in some of the worst romances, merely the passive victims of circumstances beyond their control, virtually spectators, and accident-prone at that.

The third rule is that of the 'invisible' author – another point

we'll be returning to. You, the author, should be like the pup-
peteer inside the Punch and Judy booth: we all know he's there
working the strings, but we don't want to see him, or the illusion is
destroyed. The voices we hear are – so we must believe – those of
Punch or Judy or the Policeman: the story is presented through
them and by them. Hence the need to know how a child thinks, as
well as how children express themselves. Which isn't easy.

Needless to say – though I will say it before someone else does
– these rules can be broken, and sometimes are successfully
broken. The wards of Mary Poppins actually do very little, and *The
Wind in the Willows* contains one beautifully lyrical chapter which
brings the action to a grinding halt and is almost incomprehen-
sible to children anyway. But in both cases the stories have exceptional qualities – though very different ones – which transcend
the rules but make them dangerous precedents to follow.

Of course not all your characters need be children. Parents,
witches and adult villains are allowed in; the protagonists themselves might be cats, come to that, or moles and, for older children, even adults – Gulliver is very much a grown-up! In these
cases you are looking at the scene through the child's eyes at one
remove, as it were; whole areas of adult or animal thought and
behaviour will need to be excluded without loss of verisimilitude.
Children's writers who achieve this difficult feat appeal at their
best to 'children of all ages': that is, to adults who haven't altogether lost their remembered innocence as well as to the young.
This may be on account of hidden levels of interpretation – everyone knows *Gulliver's Travels* was a political satire, and some ultra-
erudite pundits have thought *Alice's Adventures in Wonderland* was
too, though of course it wasn't – but your story must succeed at
the topmost and obvious level or it won't succeed at all.

Stories for older children and especially older boys – adventure stories – come close to novels for boys-of-all-ages anyway.
When I took my wife and our small daughter to see the film *Chitty-*

Chitty-Bang-Bang I remarked knowledgeably that it was by the author of the James Bond novels; to which my wife replied even more knowledgeably, 'Well, of course. After all, it's very similar, isn't it.' And of course it is. The Bond car, instead of having built-in machine guns and Boadicea-type scythes sprouting out of the wheel hubs, now goes a step further: it spreads wings and flies. The difference is only one of degree.

From the material or business angle, however, there are some marked differences. For the average juvenile book you must expect less cash 'up front' by way of an advance and a lower royalty scale (see Agreements on page 153) than for a an average adult book. This is because children's books for traditional rather than logical reasons have to be sold at a lower price, the assumption being that children have less spending money, though it's usually adults who pay for them. It is also, if anything, more difficult to place a new juvenile than an adult book, partly because the children's editors who take them on (or don't) tend to have pretty subjective ideas of what they are convinced children like and partly because children even more than adults go for authors rather than titles or titillating jackets. (This, like many things in this book, is arguable, but I'm drawing on my experience of both bookselling and children.)

As against these gloomy predictions, there are distinct advantages once the book is launched, and some children's books such as Roald Dahl's and J.K. Rowling's Harry Potter books have become internationally famous and enjoyed undreamt-of success. Children's books seldom date and, with luck, won't go out of print and disappear within a year or even six months, as adult books have a tendency to do. Because, remember, every year produces a whole new crop of readers of the appropriate age group. Also, there is the happy thought that parents buy their children books they themselves enjoyed in their youth. Such books, if popular with lots of parents – and the children who go on to become parents in turn – become classics. Few adult books do. I am still collecting on behalf of my authors of children's books royalties on titles published twenty or more years ago. Writers of children's books seldom get rich quick, or get rich at all – some have, as we see – but a growing number of books that stay in print over the years can produce a useful income almost *ad infinitum* or at least until copyright runs out.

Books for the very young are mostly picture books, in which case the artist will be at least as important as the author. If that's the case, the writer's remuneration will be lower still, very likely halved, the other half going to the artist. Even if the artist settled for an outright fee, the cost will be taken into account and set against the author's share of the spoils. This is disagreeable, and the ideal plan would be to illustrate it yourself, like Beatrix Potter, in the none-too-likely event that your drawings, paintings or photographs are up to professional standards. Next best would be to work in tandem with an illustrator friend, presenting the publisher with the complete package. (This way you would also like the illustrations; otherwise you might hate them. Tough. There's probably nothing you can do about it.) Agents will be unenthusiastic otherwise, because if the publisher produces the illustrator and your fee is halved, so is his commission, though not his work.

There is one class of books which may or may not belong to this section but which deserves a tentative mention: young adult books. They supposedly bridge the gap for, I suppose, younger teenagers who wouldn't be seen dead with a child's book – and haven't reached the age when they go back to them, perhaps on the excuse of reading them to other children – and aren't quite ready, in theory at least, for the sex and mayhem of the adult reading world. It's an ill-defined class, especially when teenagers are becoming more and more sophisticated and knowing; personally I'm not sure that the concept ever worked successfully, though it still exists. I once handled an adult historical novel full of rape and horrors which was subsequently published in the USA where, somewhat to my amazement, it was seized by a book club for their young adult section. (Having subsequently come across many teenage magazines, I am less amazed.) I dare say, though, that not a few adult authors of previous generations, such as Rider Haggard, would today make excellent young adult fiction.

Some young adult books, written for series, deal with the problems and dilemmas of youth today. This is fine and results in some splendid novels; but, less happily, the problems of youth in Britain are not necessarily the problems of youth in North America and elsewhere, and you may find yourself limited to the UK market.

For short stories in volume form see Collected Stories on page 87.

The novel

> Fictitious prose narrative of volume length portraying
> characters and actions representative of real life in
> continuous plot.*

That's the *Concise Oxford Dictionary* having a pretty good stab at a definition; but it doesn't include Tolkien, say, or much of science fiction, unless we allow an awful lot of latitude to real life. And I'd hate to be asked what length constitutes a volume. (Paul Gallico's *Small Miracle*, published as a book, is undeniably a short story, and I can think of many more oddities including novels published in more than one volume – but don't try it today.) In practice the range is so wide, and its boundaries continually stretched still wider by experimental work, that I doubt a definition covering every possibility is feasible without being so loose as to be meaningless. Nevertheless, by a little judicious cheating we may con-

---

* A later edition – perhaps wisely – omitted the last eleven words

veniently, if not altogether accurately, divide novels into two classes: the category and the non-category.

Category novels are those that come under such useful headings as adventure, bodice ripper, crime, detection, espionage, family stories, fantasy (sword and sorcery), feminist, fictionalized biography, gay, ghost, historical, literary, occult, romantic, saga, science fiction, sex and shopping, thriller, war, whodunit and young adult, though these categories have become far less clear-cut of late. As you will readily see, these often overlap anyway. There is also now an unabashed Erotic market for novels written for and by women, and a number of general publishers have introduced a separate imprint for these, generally in original paperback, though not a few modern novels take the erotic as far if not further.

I mentioned that the female-targeted erotic novels are usually published in paperback, but first novels which used to appear in hardback and then, if successful, in paperback up to a year later now increasingly appear originally in paperback and attract reviewers and, as we've seen, libraries in the same way as hardcovers.

There is also a label marked 'general' – this is the cheating bit – which is usually applied to non-fiction, but I offer it here for novels on less specific themes that nevertheless follow conventional lines without too many departures. One could go on inventing labels, but the point is, if you can invent a label, you are thinking of one of the traditional novel formats, broadly recognizable, and this is helpful to everybody.

It helps the author by providing signposts set up by his predecessors to show where he ought to be heading, even if he frequently deviates from too well-trodden a path. It is as foolish to ignore the rich traditions of English literature, or even the fly-by-night successes, as it is to design a building ignoring anything ever built before, whether it's a cowshed or a cathedral.

It helps the publisher because he will – if you've chosen intelligently or luckily – have published something similar before, which was either a success or it wasn't. (You can guess how this will affect his decision on yours; but the fact is, some publishers are better at selling some types of fiction than others, and it's in your interest to be taken on by the right one.) The publisher's sales force will be familiar with the right outlets, and his rights people will know the likely paperback houses and book clubs – if your novel is following a successful trend.

And it helps the potential book buyer, naturally, who will know from browsing whether or not it's the kind of novel he (or Aunt Flossy if it's a present) generally likes.

Anything that stubbornly resists having any label attached to it is non-category. The publisher brave or rash enough to take it on will have problems. His publicity department and sales force will have a daunting task trying to explain and promote it. Thus, non-category novels seldom get a warm welcome. I know one publisher whose eminently practical formula for a good, commercial novel is this: something that can be described on a newspaper headline. No non-category novel could. Of those that get in by the side door – bought by an untrained or else exceptionally perceptive editor – a remarkably high percentage end up as bestsellers and, occasionally, start a new cult. If a non-category novel is what you have in mind, I've no guidelines to offer; and if I had you would ignore them anyway.

In all probability your novel will be category; not because you are writing to a formula – though you may be: read on – but because your plot, theme or idea will almost certainly fit into one of the category groups mentioned. Or into a combination of two or more. For some reason certain combinations which look as if they should blend don't: science fiction/humour is dodgy, though I've sold several, science fiction addicts being disinclined to see the funny side; the romantic/whodunit has probably had its day. If you are, then, plotting a category novel – and it isn't easy to think of a non-category plot – you should once again be aware of the rules, even if you don't stick to them. It isn't possible to attempt more than a sampling, but a glance at some of the more popular types may give you a pattern which, with a little imagination, can be applied to others.

Do bear in mind – it seems worth while repeating it here – that the basis of any fictional plot is conflict.

The general novel

A young writer, slaving away at her first novel, was introduced at a party to a publisher and buttonholed him: 'Tell me, what is the length of the average novel?' to which he replied offhand, 'Oh about eighty thousand words.' 'Thank God!' she cried. 'I've finished.' Which introduces the vexed question of length. The publisher's answer to an unanswerable question was as sensible as any answer to an unanswerable question can be: a reasonable minimum. but in fact unlike non-fiction (where you're bound to run out of facts sooner or later) and certain more precise categories of fiction, the general novel can be any length the author chooses to make it. You will surely be aware that many bestselling novels, such as *Gone with the Wind*, *The Far Pavilions* or *The Lord of the Rings*, have been very, very long. You might assume from this fact that very, very long novels are what publishers want most.

Not true.

The first thing a publisher does when faced with a hefty great MS which he likes is to calculate how much of it can be cut out. In fairness, nearly all novels can be improved by skilful cutting. My agency has had several novels republished in the *Reader's Digest* series of Condensed Books, usually about three in one volume, greatly reduced in length with virtually nothing of importance missing from the text; but that isn't the primary consideration here. The primary consideration is cost. You don't need to be an expert to appreciate that a long novel is going to cost more to produce – in terms of paper, printing and editorial work – than a short one; or that the initial investment has to be recovered either by slapping a higher price on the finished book – perhaps so much higher as to make it unsaleable – or by printing a tremendous number of copies from the start, which will bring the price down again. The latter is, of course, the answer; provided the copies in the tremendous first printing are actually sold – which doesn't always happen. In a word – risk. The publisher's risk is greatly increased.

None of this should deter you from writing a mammoth saga if that's what you've set your heart on and the length is justified, as in a saga it usually is. A short novel should to some extent stand a better chance, but it has to be said that in either case the publishers' prime consideration today is whether or not they can envisage substantial sales. And this is why my own first novel would stand little chance, its sales correctly anticipated at about 2,000 maximum, thus producing a very modest profit for author and publisher, most of whom won't be looking for modest profits today. Exceptions are lovely – the publisher who doesn't see it as a potential blockbuster but nevertheless likes your work and is prepared to take a cautious gamble on your future – but sadly rare.

It isn't possible to give precise hints on the putting together of a general novel, which by definition is imprecise; I can at best pass on what I happen to think are the most common mistakes this type is especially prone to (see Getting It Right on page 29).

The first chapter, and indeed the first page, is your shop window. An experienced publisher's reader is reported as saying that if the first dozen pages didn't inspire her she gave up. I pointed this out to one new novelist, to which he crossly replied that it isn't the shop window that's important but what's in the shop. True, but it's the window that entices the potential buyer into the shop in the first place or doesn't. George Meredith claimed to make his early chapters deliberately difficult as 'signposts to warn the dull-witted' to follow him no further. Unfortunately it wasn't only the dull-witted who took the hint. Put it another way, in the words of that that supreme craftsman P.G. Wodehouse on the problems of where to start a novel (or, as he put it, 'this dashed difficult problem of where to begin it'):

> It's a thing you don't want to go wrong over, because one false step and you're sunk. I mean, if you fool about too long at the start, trying to establish atmosphere, as they call it, and all that sort of rot, you fail to grip and the customers walk out on you.*

Unfortunately, a lot of beginners – and also some practised hands – do 'fool about too long at the start'. Not only by trying to establish atmosphere but more commonly by desperate efforts to get as many of the cast as possible on stage for the opening scene. (*The Forsyte Saga*, in my opinion crassly underrated by some modern critics whose own novels are much inferior, is arguably guilty of this.) In some cases, for example, the reader is bombarded with endless facts about these people, their ages, backgrounds, relationships, before he or she has had a chance to get to know them individually, let alone remember who the hell they are when they pop up again in Chapter 3. You know the feeling. You stop short and thumb crossly back through the pages. Was Dickon the one with red hair who's married to Samantha? Is Mary-Lou Dirk's wife or his mother? All you're told is that when he came home she kissed him and got his supper.

If you look back and see that you've done this, a useful tip is to scrap the first chapter (or two) and make Chapter 2 (or 3, as the

---

* *Right Ho, Jeeves*

case may be) your new Chapter 1. Because by then you will have got into your swing. Some adjustment will of course be necessary, but you may be surprised to find how easily that can be done. Very often a later chapter makes an excellent opening to the book.

I do offer one golden rule for a first novel. We have already considered shop windows, 'establishing an atmosphere' and multiple characters, but consider what I call the Read On Factor. Even if the MS comes with a synopsis, the first and probably crucial reader will start at page one of a properly presented MS with no idea what to expect. Open with something dramatic, which usually means *something happening*. A classic example, and one of my favourites, is Alan Paton's *Cry the Beloved Country*, which opens with: 'The lieutenant was on Pretorius Street when he heard the sound of feet running.' He goes on to say that: 'Pretorius Street is in the . . . of South Africa', but we already want to know; we're interested. Or Daphne du Maurier's *Rebecca*: 'Last night I dreamed I went to Manderley again.' Though in the narrator's thoughts, it is still happening, immediately drawing the reader into the story. Both these are examples where the reader is compelled to *read on*, to want to know what comes next. Once you've done that it may not, of course, guarantee acceptance, but you are in the running. Novels that ignore this are usually those written some time ago or are by established 'names' who can ignore almost any rules.

Look at your MS again.

I must add here, if only to protect my rear, that it's neither wrong nor impossible to open with a massive cast. But it does call for quite formidable skills as ringmaster to keep them all under control at once. To play safe, I'd recommend introducing one or two characters to be going on with and to let them, so to speak, sink in. Don't forget to describe them, so the reader has a mental picture. The skilled novelist will make it as brief as possible, while still leaving a strong and positive image that remains in the reader's mind, like someone really striking briefly introduced at a party; you'll get to know them better in due course. Delineation of character is best handled by degrees and absorbed slowly by the reader. As all romantic novelists know, this can be an excellent way of deliberately creating wrong first impressions; keeping back a few surprises for the reader later on. Try to write a 'first impression' rather than a potted biography. (This applies to scenes and places too. A country house might be better introduced into your story as 'a mass of grey stone rising above the trees' – in the manner of an impressionist painter – rather than by a stone-by-stone description.)

You are allowed to tell the reader this yourself, at least to kick off, but the less you use this ploy the better. The 'invisible author' rule applies here, unless you are yourself the narrator (see First Person Singular on page 44). Otherwise, let one of your characters do the talking and explaining for you, even if he's talking to himself. It's fair to describe Fran as incredibly beautiful if it's in the course of mentioning that she is a supermodel: it's then a fact and a relevant one. By itself, it's an opinion – yours, the author's. Information like this should appear almost accidental, or incidental, as if it chanced to come out in the course of the narrative, not deliberately introduced.

Dialogue is of course an enormous help in establishing character. Imagine you are writing a play for radio, where the only clue as to who is speaking is the voice itself, but also the tricks of expression, the way the character habitually expresses himself or herself. That's a tough test but worth keeping in mind.

Having divided novels into two classes, let's divide the general novelist's material into two classes too: the bits he or she enjoys and looks forward to writing and the tiresome bits in between necessary for continuity, to keep the show on the road. The first are called 'set pieces' and the second 'bridging passages'. You know the sort of thing. The set pieces are the highlights – in operatic terms the arias – the memorable bits everywhere else is leading up to. In a novel it might be the show-down, the rape or even when Charles learns that he's been made redundant. They should be dramatic, the degree of drama depending on what sort of novel you're writing, which we'll come to. The bridging passages should be kept as brief as possible, conveying the needful information without losing interest. It might be preferable to say, 'It was autumn before he saw Lynn again', rather than plough through all the things he did through the winter, spring and summer. If it's not immediately relevant to your story it's probably best left out or briefly indicated rather than explained at length.

The literary novel

It's tempting to lump this together with the general novel since they have much in common, except that not all general novels by any means are literary, in the sense that they depend to a lesser extent on fine writing or profundity; more likely on a good old-fashioned plot or story. In the literary novel one expects the interest to depend more on the delineation of character in depth and less on the 'action'. This can be every bit as effective. If the reader strongly identifies with the characters to the extent of empathy, even relatively trivial events which affect them personally can have a dramatic impact. At this point the reader really cares.

Presenting characters at this level usually involves the use of 'internal' dialogue, revealing the inmost thoughts and emotions, 'getting inside' the protagonist. I would go further, stick my neck out and say that in all literary novels (and some others) the true drama which carries the thing and makes it memorable is invariably emotional rather than physical (think of *Wuthering Heights*).

The adventure novel

In this category – which includes allied classes such as most espionage, thriller, and some horror and war stories – the balance swings the other way. It depends on action, pace, storyline and excitement. For this very good reason, though strong, easily identifiable characters are a plus, they are secondary to the plot, in that they need not be explored in depth. Generally their character will be delineated in terms of what they do and, secondly, say, not what they think – in emotional terms. (Of course they can think what they're going to do next or puzzle out clues.) Internal dialogue here is undesirable if it holds up the action, and in all probability it will. A thriller should thrill. Here, especially, bridging passages must never run into *longueurs*. Don't tempt the reader to skip, as he assuredly will, to find out what happens next.

Which is not to say that cardboard, two-dimensional characters will do. You can still present them in mainly physical terms and make them believable without delving into their psyches: Clint Eastwood rather than Kenneth Branagh.

Science fiction

This is a genre most susceptible to getting the balance wrong between character and story or more probably background: in this case gadgets. New writers of science fiction run the risk of being carried away by their own ingenuity, and we are back – if you haven't been skipping the sections you don't think apply to you – to mountains and mountaineers. However ingenious your invented technology is, without live people to relate to it the result can be about as inspiring as a handbook on nuclear physics. The science bit is the background, the stage setting the backcloth. It's not quite the same fighting Things from Outer Space or animated vegetables as it is fighting Red Indians or SMERSH; but it's not much use either having a terrific backcloth with no real actors in front.

The romantic novel

Let's look at the *Concise Oxford Dictionary* again. Romance? 'A literary genre with romantic love or highly imaginative unrealistic episodes forming the central theme.' I imagine a number of female editors who deal with this class of fiction might take umbrage at 'unrealistic', as they are often supposed to represent everyday life; but, to be honest, only in the sense that the settings do. Which of course is the heart of the matter: escapism from just that. The reader after all doesn't want to read about a life just like hers – usually hers – as it is; she wants to read about a life something like hers as it – by a series of miracles – might be. (Don't we all?)

Another slightly spurious division: 'upmarket' and 'downmarket'. The upmarket classification, to take them in reverse order of importance, covers romantic love stories which, by virtue of their delineation of character in depth and sticking rather close to this realistic business, could be called 'serious' and edge into the general novel class. They are usually the longer ones.

The downmarket types are not – let's face it – too serious, which is to say believable. This is not to knock them; they are undoubtedly among the most popular novels of the whole range of fiction and can be among the most lucrative. Nor are downmarket romances the only ones that are unrealistic. I doubt if I need to quote examples from other classes which have hit the bestseller lists. All I mean is the sort of novel you believe in, if the author is skilful, while you are reading it – by a process known as 'suspension of disbelief' – but afterwards have to admit highly unlikely. Does that matter? Not at all. It's a tribute to the author's skill.

We noted in the section on occasional writing that it is possible but unlikely that a short story written with no particular market in mind would find a home, and this is equally true of the romantic novel. Just as with what used to be the traditional women's-magazine stories of which they are an extension, they need to fit a tried and tested pattern or formula. Indeed, some of the most successful publishers of these light novels provide their own formulas which they will send you on request, not only stipulating the length but also the age range, backgrounds and motives of the main characters and limiting their number. This sounds as if they are virtually writing the story for you, but in practice there are infinite possible variations. The old, primary plot for a magazine story was boy-meets-girl, boy-loses-girl, boy-gets-girl-back-again, and it's still hard to beat, except that it now reads girl-meets-boy, hates him and subsequently discovers him to be very loveable – and usually rich. I'm sure I'm not giving away too many trade secrets if I add that the villain-hero is more often than not an updated version of Heathcliff.

Because the romantic novel has been so popular and success-ful, especially in the paperback market – which, as we have seen, has now taken the place of the hardback library outlet – there is tremendous competition, and the standard in its class is high; which is to say, highly professional.

The historical novel
This may overlap the romantic of course. Romantic historicals have been out of fashion of late, but there are signs of a recovery. Successful writers in the historical genre frequently stick to one period of history, for the best of reasons: in order to write a histor-ical novel you need to familiarize yourself with the period, whether it be Regency or biblical or whatever. You will, or should, read widely and perhaps fill notebooks with details of what they wore and ate, how they travelled, major historical events of the time and anything else you can lay your hands on that relates to life as it was then lived. When the information isn't available, for very early periods perhaps, you have to use your imagination, but that in turn will be guided by historical probabilities – or at least possibilities. Imagination shouldn't be unbridled. Hence, once you have mugged up on your period, most of the background will be there, ready and waiting for your next novel.

Dialogue needs especial attention. The farther you go back in history, the less you will be able to use the speech of the age, even if you know what it looked or sounded like. Your best course, in that event, will be to invent a turn of speech, conveying if you can the flavour of the age and producing something credible to the reader which is neither modern nor unintelligible or difficult to follow. Too many 'Gadzooks' or 'Sayest thou so's?' will become indigestible. (I discovered this for myself when writing a biblical novel in the English, more or less, of James I, full of 'thee' and 'thou'. This worked well enough in brief dialogue, but the matching construction couldn't be sustained without getting stilted. I compromised.)

Try to keep in tune with the customs of the time and place in so far as you are able, which means soaking up all you can of the real background. Authors can and do get away with anachronisms, but it's hardly to be recommended unless you're deliberately writing some sort of parody. In one successful American biblical novel published not so long ago, Joseph was represented as a sort of Midwestern farmer, who paused in his ploughing to take off his hat and bang it against his knee to mop his brow. In the Middle East they didn't wear hats in New Testament times, and still don't.

The historical accuracy will depend on the level at which you are aiming, but accuracy is always a plus. However, don't fall into the same trap as with science fiction by letting your historical background come overmuch to the fore. *Gone with the Wind* is all about the American Civil War, but what we remember is the love story of Scarlett and Rhett.

Historical periods come and go in and out of favour with publishers – and presumably the reading public, though I've never understood why public taste should change overnight. It's worth checking if you can. Don't follow well-known authors, who already have a following and can ignore trends, which you can't. At the time of writing this, Regency novels are still out of fashion in Britain but not in the USA, and so indeed are most historicals other than the sexy ones commonly known as 'bodice rippers' – a term which speaks for itself. But there are, as usual, frequent exceptions. An outstanding novel in this area – whether literary or plainly commercial – may turn out a blockbuster, and not a few have.

Crime

There is a perennial market for good crime and detection novels, which seldom hit the high spots, though of course some do, but have a more or less guaranteed and quite healthy sale. Because this is so, the competition here, too, is fairly stiff and the standard high. An unusual background knowledge can help considerably, as with Dick Francis. Length should generally be kept down to around 80,000 words, or less, though there will always be exceptions. Again, they can slip into the literary category; P.D. James is one author whose work bridges the two.

Collected stories

These are more commonly found in books for children because for some reason – apart from the classics and the inevitable exceptions – adults can't be persuaded to buy collections of short stories in volume form, even by well-known novelists; original ghost stories are an exception, perhaps because they are rare, and I would say the same goes for horror stories and science fiction, at least in original paperback. However, as much the same rules apply to children's and to adult stories, I've lumped them together.

They need not of course be 'collected' in the sense of having been previously published elsewhere, like verse: they can be original to the book. Nor need they necessarily be fiction.

The first essential is for the stories, or non-fiction essays, to have a strongly recognizable linking theme. (Collections by well-known short story writers such as Guy de Maupassant and Somerset Maugham are excluded of course.) With ghost or horror the theme is already there. Otherwise, it may be the same central character running through the book in self-contained 'episodes' instead of the normal chapters; the Sherlock Holmes stories are examples of this. The best collections make ideal bedside reading, for children and adults alike. Generally, though, a collection is a tough proposition to make a start with. When you have published several reasonably successful novels or non-fiction works, and have built up a following, your publisher may feel more charitably inclined.

Collections by various hands again invariably have a connecting theme, gathering together in one volume stories or essays by authors already known as good of their kind or occasionally simply producing something suitable for the formula. Nevertheless, there appear regular collections on certain themes, horror especially, whose editors will willingly consider work from newcomers. Indeed, some publishers look out for new authors by this method.

5 Helping hands

Of course you may lock yourself up in your room and write your book all by yourself, entirely from your imagination. More probably, even if it's fiction you're writing, you will need to consult other books, maps, travel brochures or whatever to get your background facts right. Quite often, though, you may need to consult other people: perhaps you need someone to do the leg work, to do research for you, tracking down facts in libraries or photographs from collections, in which case they will have to be paid for their services. These days, of course, you can do much of this yourself using the Internet.

Occasionally your helpers will be required to do more: to assist in the actual writing or preparation of your book, in which case their contribution becomes a major one and you will need to know how to cope with it.

Let's look at the two most likely instances.

Ghosts – literary

Some psychic people can see ghosts where ordinary folk can't, which is nicely paralleled by the relationship between the ostensible author of a ghosted book and the ghost-writer who actually did the writing.

If you have a good story to tell but lack the skill, time or inclination to write it up yourself, you may employ a professional writer to put the words together. Strictly speaking the book will then appear under your name, and the 'ghost' will be satisfied with whatever payment you have agreed for his services and will disappear in the way ghosts tend to. Less strictly speaking, the ghost will sometimes be additionally rewarded by a credit in the prelims – the preliminary pages before the beginning of the text – 'Without whose assistance . . .' And sometimes indeed, especially in the case of celebrities' 'autobiographies', the book will be described as 'By . . . as told to/with . . .' In which case the ghost isn't really a ghost at all but a co-author.

In any case the ghost will have to be paid, either by a lump sum or by a share of whatever the book earns or by a combination of the two. The as-told-to quasi-ghost may specialize in this kind of work, become well known for it and be much sought after. This is the most expensive kind of ghost and will cost you a substantial fee or up to half of your earnings.

Whether the ghost will accept a share of the proceeds as remuneration or not depends on the book's prospects. If you have an enthusiastic publisher already lined up, your ghost will be willing to share the risk with you. If you haven't and publication is uncertain, he probably won't, and you can't blame him.

In effect, you will get what you pay for, unless you're unusually lucky with bargains or are on particularly friendly terms with the ghost. A modest fee may be accepted by a competent 'hack', who may well do a good job. A really skilled ghost-writer will be busy – very likely writing a book of his own – and won't take time off unless it's worth his while. As with co-authors, you will need a collaboration agreement before you get down to work.

Another possibility is that, if you're famous or infamous, a ghost may approach you. An agent will sometimes be able to find a ghost for you, but he will generally need to be convinced that your story is a viable one.

Collaborations and co-authors

Instead of writing and presenting a book all by yourself, you may decide to work in collaboration with A.N. Other: possibly more than one other. There could be a number of reasons for this. Perhaps your collaborator is someone close to you – husband, wife, partner – and you've been sharing ideas. Or it could be that, while you have considerable knowledge of your subject, there are gaps here and there which your collaborator is eminently well qualified to fill. If you are writing a book for children or any book which needs illustrating – a technical book, for instance – you may team up with an artist whose work perfectly complements your text, so much so that his or her work becomes more or less as important as yours. In which case, if you plan to present the publisher with the complete package, instead of paying the artist a fee, you may wish to share the proceeds. In any of these cases, you are forming a partnership. In a publishing agreement you will be lumped together as the 'Author', or 'Proprietor'; that is, joint owners of the original copyright. Before you come to the publishing agreement, however, you have to reach agreement between yourselves.

First, you need to settle on the method of working: who is going to do what – fairly obvious if you're working with an artist. Then, on the basis of how the work is shared out, how are you going to split the profits? Fifty–fifty if you are each putting in an equal amount of time and effort, or pro rata if not. But there are other considerations: for example, one of you may have the established name which will launch the book or one may have conceived the original idea. If an agent is involved he will advise you, but only you and your collaborator can finally decide.

Unless you are a husband-and-wife team or something similar, you would be wise to get the terms of your partnership down in writing, in the form of a simple collaboration agreement. If you are good and close friends you may think this unnecessary. So did I, until one of my collaborating authors unfortunately died, which meant that his share went to his next of kin: his wife. But the woman in question had omitted to go through the legal process of marrying him, perhaps because he was married already to another woman, who now presented herself, so to speak, out of the blue and, in the absence of a formal agreement, claimed his share for herself.

Your agent, if you have one, will prepare a collaboration agreement for you, in the form of your joint instructions to him as to how you want the spoils divided. The publisher won't be involved, since all moneys go to the agent anyway and whom he pays afterwards is none of the publisher's business. The collaboration agreement should state whether one is or both are to hold the copyright, because it's the copyright holder who is authorized to sign contracts (it could be a nuisance if there were three of you and all three had to be consulted before any deal was made), arrangements for recouping out-of-pocket expenses (such as photocopying), an undertaking perhaps that neither of you will be involved in writing a book of a similar nature in competition with this one for a given period and any other specific limitations relevant to the particular work. With an author–artist collaboration you might want to specify that if either the text or the artwork alone is used in some sort of spin-off, the cash split will be adjusted.

If you have no agent and you hold copyright jointly, you may simply instruct the publisher to pay each of you whatever percentages you have agreed on. If it gets more complicated you may need to consult a solicitor and have him draw up the agreement as a last resort (see Lawyers on page 166)

6 Writing down and freewheeling

Your aim is to write – beautifully – a work of great erudition that will establish your name among the literary gods on the higher slopes of Parnassus and will be a lasting contribution to English Literature. (It would be nice if it made you some money, too, of course.)

Good for you.

Unfortunately, none of the publishers you've tried (an obtuse lot) has appreciated the immense potential of your work. They have said agreeable things about it but added with regret that they didn't believe they would be able to sell a sufficient number of copies to pay the printing bill, let alone you, on account of there not being enough people out there (an even more obtuse lot) remotely likely to buy it. In other words, it's not 'commercial'.

So you look about you to see what is.

Right. You will write something commercial. Then, once you've made a name for yourself – and lots of money – you will write what you really want to write.

If that sounds like you, do be careful.

Perhaps, though, I'm insulting you. Perhaps you have failed to find a home for your *magnum opus* and it's dawned on you that it isn't after all up to something mysteriously called 'professional standard'. You aim at a nearer and bigger target. In fact, an easy one. You try going downmarket. (This applies particularly to the magazine and book light-romance markets.) If others can write this light, knockabout stuff, you certainly can.

Conscious – or even unconscious – of writing now way below your peak, you'll be tempted to think almost any old thing will do and, as we've said, it's easy.

It won't and it isn't.

If you are literate and fluent it's often easier to let your imagination have its head than to work within the limits of a tight discipline. It's the difference between sitting on a horse and letting it go where it fancies at a pace of its own choosing and making the brute do what you want it to. The first may provide a thoroughly enjoyable and perhaps exciting ride, but it isn't good horsemanship, and it's no fun for anyone trying to follow you. The same applies to what we may call – to change the metaphor from horses to bicycles – literary freewheeling.

The truth is, there is good and bad writing at all levels, and the good equals the professional. And it is very difficult, if not quite impossible, to produce solid professional work if you don't believe in what you're writing.

It shows. If you find you are condescending to write below what you feel is your natural level it's going to show; and you are, in effect, insulting the reader. The reader will know this; or rather he would if it ever got beyond the editor, which it won't.

If you find yourself writing down, change tack and approach it from another angle. Some of the 'light' stuff is really quite enjoyable. See if you can't seriously do it a little better. You just could find yourself enjoying it. You could even find it is what you really, in your heart of hearts, wanted to write all along. If you turn out to be good at it, you wouldn't be the first.

Stage 2

Presenting Your Work

7 Setting it out

The time spent in setting your work out in its final form for publication will be negligible compared with the time and trouble involved in its creation, and yet all too often authors rush this last fence, either from ignorance, arrogance or exhaustion, ignoring the importance of first impressions. But first impressions are important and, while they don't guarantee acceptance, they should ensure a sympathetic reading. Give your work the best chance you can.

The manuscript
Strictly speaking, the manuscript is something written *manu*, by hand, which almost nobody will be prepared to consider these days: typescript would be the proper word. Both terms are used in the trade, but as manuscript, with its familiar contraction to MS, is the more usual one, that's what we'll call it. If you use a typing agency or freelance typist, make sure whoever does it is accustomed to typing authors' MSS. Not all are. Personal recommendation by another author is best, but failing that look for advertisements in one of the literary journals, such as *The Times Literary Supplement* or the *London Review of Books*. An immaculate MS won't sell a poor literary work, and a poor one won't necessarily be fatal to its chances, but first impressions are important, and you don't want to create needless obstacles for yourself.

These days the usual metric size of paper in the UK is A4, the normal, full-sized business letter, and, unless you have good and valid reasons for varying it, don't. Use normal weight; paper that is too thick makes a MS bulky, expensive to post and look longer than it is, which could be a disadvantage. Paper that is too flimsy gets tatty quickly and may be near-transparent, so the reader has to lift the page to avoid seeing the following page through it: another cause of irritation. White paper is usual. Curiously, pale yellow, which presents less of an eye strain, isn't, but there is no objection to it. Use a black record ribbon or cartridge on a word processor; you need red only for play scripts. Clearly, using a PC eliminates most problems and these days a computer is pretty much the norm. Even university students are expected to have their work word-processed. But don't go over the top with fancy or mixed typefaces!

Leave fairly generous margins; say 4cm (1½ inches) on the left-hand side – so that if the MS is bound every page remains accessible and legible when opened out to the last – with about 2.5cm (1 inch) on the right-hand side. If the MS is much handled and pages curl or fray, the right-hand side can be guillotined leaving a clean edge with the text unaffected. The same applies to the top and bottom – especially the bottom: elderly typewriters, if you are still using one, usually drift dejectedly downwards if you get too near the baseline, like unwatered plants. And, anticipating the book's being bought by a publisher, there must be room for editorial and design marks.

It's preferable to have three copies, because you may sometimes have to submit two copies of a manuscript, and you need one for your files. Again, a word processor or PC will print out as many copies as you like and retain the text on the hard drive. Or you can photocopy.

Typing should be on one side of the paper only and double-spaced, that is with twice the normal interval between lines (not, of course, between words, which I *have* come across). Don't use CAPITAL LETTERS for whole words unless that's how you want them to appear in print. I would say never for emphasis. Emphasis is conveyed by italics – easy on a modern computer but, if using a typewriter, you underline the words you want italicized.

Be consistent in your spelling of names and your use of capital letters (see House Style on page 179).

Don't leave an extra line space (twice the double-spacing you are otherwise using) in between paragraphs unless you mean to indicate a sort of sub-chapter, as for instance a change of scene. This very common mistake makes a MS look twice as long and makes a word count well nigh impossible.

Indent at the beginning of each new paragraph, always remembering that a change of speaker in dialogue calls for a new paragraph no matter how short (like one word) the previous bit of dialogue was (see Dialogue on page 45). This is not an absolute rule, but otherwise if the previous text runs to the end of its line there's nothing to indicate a new paragraph.

However, the short rule of thumb for setting out a page of, say, a novel is simply this: open any conventional novel almost anywhere and copy the layout, only with double-spacing instead of single, and underlining, if necessary, for italics, and there you have it. I say a novel because novels have dialogue, but the same applies for any normal book, and short stories are set out in the same way in MS, though they may appear in columns in magazines.

Number the pages of your MS consecutively. This is so obvious; the only reason I mention it is because not all authors do. I was once reading a MS with loose unnumbered pages when the cat jumped on my lap and upset the lot on the floor. Half an hour later, having murderously reassembled it, I found I had a page over. But there are other reasons for pagination, as it's called. It will not only enable you or whoever reads it to understand at once if a page is missing or misplaced, and make possible quick reference in discussions with an editor, it will also make a word count infinitely easier if you aren't using a computer.

Even if you are not writing to a specified length – which you will be with a short story, article and certain types of novels – you will need to know roughly how many words your MS runs to. (In the trade, length is measured in thousands of words. It's useless quoting how many pages, since pages vary considerably, even in books.) You calculate by averaging the number of words to a full line (count a dozen lines and divide by twelve), multiplying by the number of lines to a page and then by the number of pages in the MS. Allow a generous margin for short lines, such as dialogue and ends of paragraphs. The publisher will calculate the number of words in the same way. (The printer or designer will later make a more exact count, known as 'casting off'.) If you add pages marked 67a, 67b, 67c, allow for these too.

It should be superfluous again to add that you should never, never part with a MS without retaining at least one copy yourself. But people do. And MSS do very occasionally get lost. Most publishers have a little footnote printed at the bottom of their letterhead disclaiming responsibility for this eventuality. I have one too.

Make sure your name and address is clearly typed on the MS – preferably on the last page also, in case the first goes astray. If you use a pseudonym, put your real name as well. Covering letters all too often become separated from their MSS, and it can be difficult to reunite the two if the names are different.

Having assembled your MS, correctly typed and set out, what next? To some extent this depends on plans for its future. If it is going to the publisher who has already commissioned your book and is eagerly awaiting the script, a stout and close-fitting envelope that won't disintegrate in the post will do fine. If, on the other hand, it is likely that it will have to run the gauntlet of numerous submissions, back and forth in the post, and be thumbed through by various hands, something more substantial is called for, to preserve it from becoming dog-eared and clearly unloved. A retype of the first and last pages will help to make it look reasonably fresh.

Generally, some form of file cover or binding is a good idea. Simplest is the envelope file cover, a stiffish folder which holds the loose pages together until it's opened at the other end but won't protect them from rough handling thereafter. A folder with flexible metal tongues that pin down or a threaded lace that knots to keep the pages together in book form is probably the best bet, provided in each case it can be easily released to replace pages that become torn or damaged or you've spilt your coffee over.

However, having said all that, I have to add that, for the first approach to publisher or agent, a brief letter together with, say, up to a dozen pages of text with a synopsis is strongly recommended. A stamped, self-addressed envelope (s.a.e.) is a must, or an International Reply Coupon if you are abroad; most agents and an increasing number of publishers insist on this. Complete MSS are usually unwelcome in the first instance because everybody gets loads and loads of them, but I have already indicated that this may be ignored with a well-presented novel, which will be less unwelcome if accompanied by a suitable s.a.e., thus not only saving postage but, almost more important, *time* (see Slush Pile on page 102).

Finally, when it comes to the full MS, make sure your name is on it and do not mark it © with the year's date or FBSR which I have often come across. The first complies with the Universal Copyright Convention – virtually worldwide and the date is the date of first *publication*. FBSR – First British Serial Rights applies to newspaper or magazine publication, whether in sequential form or 'one-shot' – not to books.

For all file covers that secure the pages you will of course need a punch to make the holes. If buying a new one, look for the kind with an adjustable slide which can be placed to different paper sizes, ensuring the holes appear centrally. If not, fold the top page of the sheaf you're about to hole and make a small crease in the dead centre on the left-hand side. If you place this in the centre of the punch – it will have a protruding tongue or mark indicating where – then all your pages will be aligned. This is an enormous help if you have, or someone else has, to remove the pages and replace them again; when stacked, the holes will be in line. It saves hours and tempers and looks neat.

Second tip. Unless you are certain your publisher is going to accept your book and publish it pretty well immediately, do not date your MS. If it goes to a number of publishers, it could be a dead give-away, advertising the fact that it's been around for ages, whereas a clean new title page and perhaps last page can make a tired old MS look quite daisy-fresh.

Read your final MS over carefully. Eliminate typing errors. If corrections are necessary, type or write them in clearly: this is what the double spacing is for. If they are numerous, retype the page. It is unforgivable to present a sloppy MS and especially a badly typed or much corrected first page, which tells the reader that while you can't be bothered to get it right you expect him to be bothered to interpret it. You can guess what sort of reaction this gets.

Finally, don't overdo the packaging. You'll see I've recommended that you take some trouble in presenting a professional MS, which means a MS that is convenient to handle, trouble-free to read and easy to adjust or amend if required. That is the aim, and it is the only aim. Some authors have their MSS permanently bound in solid book form, with stiff covers and their names and the title in gold lettering (called 'brasses') down the spine. They look impressive, but for some curious reason I can't explain are never any good. It's almost as if the authors know that this is as near as they are going to get to a commercial publication.

The slush pile

This is the popular term for the accumulation of unsolicited MSS which – despite warnings in reference books, which not all new authors consult – publishers and agents regularly receive, the 'pile' usually landing on or beside the desk of an in-house 'reader', whose unenviable job it is to wade through it, discarding anything he or she knows is unsuitable for their list. As we've seen, this probably includes well-written and eminently publishable novels with nothing 'going for' them – in the publisher's reader's opinion, though many have famously been proved to be wrong – to lift them into that indefinable quality that spells likely extensive sales. The fortunate one or two that do qualify will then be passed on to the director or editor-in-chief, who will actually read it and decide whether or not to publish. It may still have to run the gauntlet of an editorial board and be dependent on whoever is championing it. As against that, the agent will (should) send a MS to the appropriate director in charge who may decide there and then. MSS from agents will normally bypass the slush pile, but I wouldn't guarantee it.

Synopses and specimen material
We've already noted that non-fiction books are regularly commissioned, meaning that the publisher undertakes to publish an as-yet unwritten book if he likes the subject or idea and is satisfied that the author will make a good job of it. Novels occasionally get commissioned too but much more rarely, unless the novelist already has an impressive track record, because whereas a biography, say, which begins well is unlikely to go madly wrong halfway through, as novels can and do.

Perhaps in your approach you've outlined your non-fiction subject in a letter, with some indications of your qualifications and why you think it a good idea – the best reason being that no one else has thought of it. In principle the publisher agrees. He will now ask you to let him have a proper synopsis or outline and, unless your previous books are very respectable, a specimen chapter or two.

The specimen chapters should be fairly straightforward. It's often best to skip the first chapter, as first chapters are often necessarily full of essential information and less exciting than later ones. Any chapter or chapters will do. Remember, what the publisher will be looking for isn't the narrative but how well you write.

The synopsis can be more tricky, especially if you haven't got the form entirely clear in your own mind; and you probably won't have, if you still have masses of research to do and don't yet know what this may turn up. To help yourself, as well as the publisher, try this:

Having at least a rough idea of the shape of your book and the way it will develop, draw up a list of chapter headings. It doesn't matter whether or not you want chapter headings in the finished book. You will then have a basic plan, framework or skeleton. It may also help you to allocate an approximate length to each chapter (in thousands of words) and from this to estimate what the length the book itself will be; you will need to do this before you sign an agreement. (If it turns out somewhat shorter or longer nobody will worry unless it's destined to fit into a series, in which case you will be told the length and will have to cut your cloth accordingly.)

Next, flesh out your skeleton by jotting down under each chapter heading the highlights of that particular section. Half a dozen lines should be quite enough. See the synopsis I wrote for my own book on the Gurkhas that follows this section.

If you do this effectively, anyone reading through your synopsis will end up with a pretty clear idea of what the book will contain – and so will you. If the publisher has also read a specimen chapter or two, he will also know how you will be presenting it, which is exactly what he wants to know at this stage.

Generally speaking, it won't matter too much if, when you get down to the actual writing, you depart from the synopsis, provided you don't stray too far.

It's worth while taking a great deal of trouble to get your specimen material as perfect as you can. This, as I've said, is your shop window, and the very best goods should be on display.

GURKHAS Synopsis

Chapter 1. LEGENDARY NEPAL
The topography of the country – early travellers' reports
from Marco Polo – the village of Gorkha, from which the
tribes were to overrun Nepal – early legends to the eighth
century – history up to the eighteenth century.

Chapter 2. THE RISE OF THE GURKHAS
The formation of the fighting clans – the influx of the Indian
Rajputs from the fall of Chitor – Prithwi Narayan's merciless
conquest – the war with the British in 1814.

Chapter 3. THE NASIRIS
The 'friendly' Gurkhas and their introduction into the
Company's forces – Hodgson's influence and diplomacy, the
'founder of Nepal' – internal strife and the rise of Jang
Bahadur – the hereditary offices of king and prime minister
– the Prince of Wales shooting in Nepal in 1876.

Chapter 4. THE GURKHA BRIGADE
The history of the Gurkha regiments in the Indian Army
from 1814 to 1914.

Chapter 5. AYO GURKHALI!
The service of the Gurkhas in the Indian Army through two
world wars – accounts of the eleven VCs won.

Chapter 6. THE BAND OF BROTHERS
Gurkhas in action post-war – the division of India and
Pakistan in 1947 – Gurkhas in the British Army – the last VC
to date in 1965 in Indonesia.

Titles and subtitles

When you write a story for a magazine, the fiction editor is generally at liberty to change the title to something he or she likes better without referring back to you. With a book your title may be changed by the publisher, after discussion, to a title that will be more saleable.

The title you put on your MS isn't binding and for ever. You can change it any time before the MS finally goes to the printer. You may discover that someone else has already used it; there is no copyright in book titles, but everyone tries to avoid duplication.

It's a matter of personal preference, but long titles can cause problems when it comes to reproducing them down the spine of a book. Still, they're not ruled out: witness Alan Sillitoe's *The Loneliness of the Long-Distance Runner*. Quotations often produce the best titles as we have seen. The chief thing to aim at is something memorable, a word of phrase the potential bookbuyer won't clean forget on the way to the bookshop. (A good bookseller should be able to help you there. In my bookselling days I was asked for *Fly the Bloody Country* and once for *A Bullet in the Belly*. No prizes for the correct titles.)

When it comes to non-fiction, your title ought to give some indication of what the book is about. I know this sounds obvious, but it isn't always easy. Apart from strictly academic books, whose titles aren't designed to be eye-catching, we're back to something memorable again. *The Primates* could equally well be about anthropology or archbishops. A subtitle, a brief phrase explaining in a nutshell what it's all about, may be, and usually is, the answer. A good example was the late H.F. Hutchison's *The Hollow Crown: The Life of Richard II*.

You can add a subtitle for fun too, if you like, or as a sort of disclaimer. Graham Greene liked to add to the title of some of his novels, the words 'An Entertainment'. (I subtitled my third novel *A Tone Poem*, for that matter, which seemed to me but to nobody else a good description; the offending words disappeared in a reprint.)

Good, effective book titles can end up as catch phrases, if they aren't already, and pass into the language, which is no bad thing for the author. Think of *Catch-22*. It's worth taking time and trouble over them, as it is over the names of your principal characters, who you hope may one day become as well known as Sherlock Holmes ('Sherlock' was an afterthought of Conan Doyle's) or Scarlett O'Hara (originally conceived as Pansy O'Hara). *Gone with the Wind* wasn't the original title, either. John Braine called his first novel *Joe for King*. Not a bad title; but *Room at the Top*, you must agree, was an improvement.

Think about it.

Pseudonyms

There are a number of reasons why you might choose to have your book published under an assumed name rather than your own.

If you happen to have been christened Frederick Forsyth, for instance, or Iris Murdoch, you would do well to avoid the inevitable confusion, even if your book is quite different from theirs. (If it is similar, you could be prosecuted for trying to pass it off as the real thing.)

You may feel that your name is too commonplace or too complicated (all those hyphens!) or unpronounceable; who is going to remember it when they ask for your book? Or, dammit, you may simply not like it.

Equally, you may not want your true identity to be revealed publicly, especially if you have a professional capacity at odds with this written work you've now produced. In which case, like Charles Lutwidge Dodgson or, more recently, Patrick O'Brien, you may think it a good idea to choose something simpler for, say, children's books. Perhaps you're simply shy.

This could also apply if you later switch from books about cats to murder mysteries, to avoid the dismay of your regular fans who seize your latest publication and are bewildered. You may want to build up a new and different readership.

It's worth while taking some trouble in choosing a pseudonym. Don't forget that if the first book is a success you're stuck with it. Many female authors hang on to their maiden names after they marry, which is again a good idea, especially if you get divorced and marry someone else.

Remember, though, that as a successful author you are likely to be interviewed in the press, on radio and television and elsewhere, which could present problems if you have a famous alter ego, though film and pop stars as well as some authors do it all the time, thus, in effect, changing their names.

8 Acknowledgements

As we shall see in a moment, some acknowledgements are manda-
tory: when copyright material is printed in your book, whether in
the text or as illustrations, for which permission has had to be
obtained, you must quote the source. But there are other
acknowledgements which, while optional, are usually very much
desirable. Many non-fiction books necessarily draw upon the work
of previous writers, and it is not only courtesy to give credit where
credit is due, it also absolves you from the suspicion of passing off
another's work or research as your own. At least equally important, it lends weight to your own conclusions and gives them
authority.

Quotations from other authors

Or for that matter from playwrights, poets, songwriters, letters or
any copyright material (see Copyright on page 162); but the bor-
rowing of authors' words is what is most likely to concern you.

If the author has been dead for at least seventy-five years, you
are in the clear – unless the work was published posthumously, in
which case copyright dates from first publication. It will be in the
public domain and anybody is free to quote from it or even to
republish the whole thing. (Don't rush off and publish the Bible in
the authorized version, however; that's Crown copyright and an
exception with no expiry.)

If you are writing a critique of another author's work, you
aren't going to get very far without quoting quite extensively

from it; but happily there is something known as fair dealing, which allows you to do so without permission (though it is strictly a privilege and not, as many suppose, a right), so long as the quotes are necessary and reasonable for your purpose, just as a book reviewer may quote freely from the book under review.

If you want to use a quote because it is appropriate to the theme of your own book – perhaps an authority to support your argument in non-fiction, or in a novel one of your characters bursts into song or verse (real song, real verse) – the first thing you must do is to trace the original source and acknowledge it. If you can't work the acknowledgement into the text you may need a footnote or a note in the prelims or an appendix. If the quotation is brief, that's all you need to do.

However, what exactly constitutes 'brief' not even a lawyer could tell you. Various attempts have been made to define it, and perhaps one day some sort of generally accepted rule will be thrashed out. Meanwhile it's a matter of custom and common sense. As a very rough guide I would suggest that formal permission is unnecessary for up to five hundred words of prose, and no more than, say, three or four lines of verse or song. Some authors and agents would quarrel with this, but personally I base it on the practical ground that the fee charged for these minimal quotes would barely cover the cost of collecting it.

The same applies to illustrations reproduced from other books or from pretty well anywhere; and some artists and photographers can be very expensive indeed (see Pictures and Illustrations on page 112).

You can paraphrase the words of other authors within reasonable limits, provided you don't try to pass the result off as your original work. There is no copyright in ideas or facts, but there may well be in the order in which they are arranged or edited and in the language in which they are expressed. Obviously, anyone paraphrasing an entire novel would be heading for trouble. Again, a clear acknowledgement of the source will generally keep you out of trouble. After all, it would be rare to produce a work of erudition without drawing upon the ideas and work of previous writers in the same field.

If in doubt, and if your quotation exceeds the meagre limits mentioned above, apply for permission. If a fee is required it will be requested (or demanded).

Fine. But how do you set about it? How on earth do you track down the author or copyright holder?

You don't need to. Write to the publisher of the book or whatever you want to quote from or reproduce. He may control quotation or reproduction rights and if he doesn't he will pass your request on to the author or whoever does.

In your letter specify exactly what you want to use, either by setting it out in full or giving the page and line numbers of the book it's from. For prose, it's additionally helpful to give the actual number of words – this will save the chap at the other end from the laborious task of counting them himself and will make him more sympathetic. In any case, if it's a book you must give the title. Next, say where your own book is to be published, that is, whether the permission you seek is for the UK and Commonwealth (which may or may not include Canada), that plus USA, or North American (that is, USA plus Canada if it's not included in with the UK and Commonwealth), and this is usually expressed as World English Language; or the World (which includes translation rights). It's preferable to cover the world, because otherwise you may have to go back and make your request all over again if your book is subsequently taken by a foreign publisher; it's also more expensive. The rights you acquire will be non-exclusive, meaning anyone else may acquire them at the same time.

It's worth while digesting these facts before you indulge in extensive quotation, because it will almost certainly fall to you, not your publisher, to write all those letters and negotiate and pay the fees – though you may be allowed cash for or towards them in addition to your advance. If you are thinking of putting together a symposium of the work of others, the research and correspondence will be formidable. But that's what you, as editor, are being paid for.

Finally, if the quotation is not too extensive, and if you have made every effort to trace the copyright holder and failed – the book may be out of print, and the publisher no longer has an interest – you are probably safe to go ahead and let the copyright holder trace you, if he becomes aware of it. In which case it is best to put a note in the prelims or acknowledgements section advertising the fact.

Pictures and illustrations

If your book requires illustrations they may be treated as part and parcel of the MS, in which case you will be expected to provide them yourself in a form suitable for reproduction. This is fine if they are photographs taken by you or at least belonging to you; if they are your own illustrations, designs or whatever, little or no expense is involved.

If, on the other hand, the pictures or illustrations need to be obtained from other sources, before signing a publishing agreement you will need to establish clearly whose responsibility it is (a) to provide them, (b) to pay reproduction fees if necessary (and this applies of course to photographs and paintings in the same way as quotations) and (c) to pay the fee for a researcher who may be needed to track down the sources and copyright holders. There is no hard and fast rule here. Sometimes the publisher will be totally responsible; sometimes the author. Quite commonly something in between the two may be agreed: the publisher may allow the author expenses up to a certain limit or simply increase the advance paid on the book to compensate for these expenses, which is a good deal less desirable since the advance is recoverable from future royalties, which expenses aren't.

If you are responsible for finding and producing the illustrations yourself and are stuck, your best bet might well be to approach one of the many picture libraries or agencies specializing in photographs. Your publisher should, however, be able to advise you in any case.

Some photographers, or copyright holders of photographs, may want to know the retail price of your book and even the print run before agreeing to a fee. In all cases where permission to reproduce pictures or illustrations is necessary, acknowledgements must be given quoting the source.

Dedications

> To the Onlie Begetter
> of these insuing Sonnets
> Mr W.H. of all Happinesse . . .

If you would like to emulate Shakespeare, and immortalize someone dear to you in the prelims of your book with something like 'To my beloved wife Mavis, without whose unflagging help this novel would have been finished in half the time', feel free. Only try to remember to include the dedication in the copy of the typescript you send to your publisher. So often the dedication is an afterthought, mentioned in a letter to the publisher when the MS has already gone to the printer, and easily mislaid or misfiled.

The same applies if you want to list your previous (if any) publications in the prelims.

Disclaimers

These are the novelists' notes in the prelims denying libel before anyone accuses them of it. You will probably have come across them though they are rarer than they used to be: 'the characters and events depicted in this novel are purely imaginary . . .' They can be unintentionally funny, like those which stoutly insist that 'the characters in this book bear no resemblance to real people, living or dead'.

Even intentionally funny. My favourite was Howard Spring's disclaimer in *Shabby Tiger* which, after the conventional denials, ended with: 'There is no such place as Manchester.'

They are intended as evidence of good faith, but won't prevent anyone who imagines he's been libelled in your book from suing you, and their legal value is negligible (but see Libel on page 163).

Stage 3
Getting It Published

9 Decision time

The novelist Elizabeth Taylor whimsically remarked that the best part of writing a book was typing the title with your name under it on the first page. 'And when you've done that, the best part is over.' If you've discovered the truth in that, then you will surely discover that the next best part is undoubtedly typing the magic words THE END.

The great day has arrived. You have completed your book in manuscript (typescript), beautifully set out and professionally presented. Or perhaps you have only decided exactly what it is you intend to write and have prepared an irresistible outline and specimen chapter or two (see Synopses and Specimen Material on page 103): not a great day, but a good one. Alternatively, you may not think much of the day at all if, as is far from uncommon, you have Misgivings. A.J. Cronin is said to have contemplated the MS of his first novel with dismay; so much so that he went out into the garden and threw it on the rubbish dump, where it got rained on. His wife rescued and ironed it: it was, of course, *Hatter's Castle*. At this point you are the worst possible judge of your own work, and the only consolation I can offer is that if it gets into print it will then look either much better or much worse. There is only one way to find out. But there are two ways of setting about it.

You can approach a publisher direct or you can try a literary agent.

Publisher or agent?

If you happen to be living abroad, the advantages of having someone on the spot and in regular touch with publishers to look after your interests may be clear: at the lowest level it will save you endless time and, if you are offering a full MS, a fortune in postage.

If this doesn't apply, it's less plain. Unless you are lucky enough to have a friend at court – a doting uncle who happens to be editorial director of Rosencrantz and Guildenstern; an established novelist who drinks at your local; even a friendly bookseller to advise you – you are on your own. (It's unfair, by the way, to ask the novelist to read your MS, which is inviting him to give up several hours of his working time for nothing. At best try a heavy hint, and don't be offended if he suddenly goes deaf in that ear, because, after all, to a professional, reading other people's MSS is work.) But let's assume that you haven't anyone to advise you, which is why you're reading this handbook. Publisher or agent, which?

As a literary agent myself, I might be presumed to come down heavily in favour of approaching an agent. But not necessarily. There are some authors who can manage very well without one. There are even more authors, not to mention would-be-authors, the agent can manage without. This doesn't have to mean they are unpublishable. It doesn't even necessarily mean the agent doesn't care for their work. It could mean that their potential sales, sufficient maybe to bring a modest profit to the publisher, would mean an actual loss to the agent working on a commission of, say, 1 or 1½ per cent of the book's selling price, especially if he has to offer the MS a number of times before it's accepted or is involved in voluminous correspondence. Expressions of regret from agents and publishers both, in rejecting your MS, may be perfectly genuine.

It has been claimed on occasion that it's as hard to find an agent as it is to find a publisher; some have said even harder. I'd say easier myself but not a lot. Both must contemplate investing time and money – which come to the same thing – not, though, at anything like the same level nor with the same level of rewards in mind. But whereas the publisher, unless he has miscalculated badly, stands at least to recover most of it, the agent if he fails to make a sale recovers nothing. Ah, you say, but that's his silly fault for taking on work he isn't damned sure of selling. True. Only if you do say that, bear it in mind when he's debating whether or not to take on yours.

Where an agent has more freedom than a publisher is the occasion when he has faith in the author's future and keeps him 'on the books', despite failures, until the right, saleable work comes up; something a publisher can't do. But there is a limit to the amount of free (in both senses) time an agent can afford to devote to this side of his work.

Publisher or agent? Having had a very brief glance at the question from the trade side, or receiving end, let's see how the choice is likely to affect the new and untried author. In basic English, what is the difference? An agency, like any other service industry, is going to charge you for its services and, as a high proportion of authors make use of these services, there's presumably something in it. It's true that there are some publishers, in the paperback houses especially, who will tell you they will consider only MSS submitted through a literary agency – and have therefore been vetted; this saves them from coping with totally impossible submissions – but most certainly won't discourage the submission of a modest sample of the proposed book (see The Manuscript on page 97).

The question I am most often asked by laymen is 'What does an agent do?' And the first answer as you may guess is 'Finds you a publisher'. (Or tries to. No agent has a 100 per cent success rate or anything approaching it. If he had, he'd be betting on certainties, which wouldn't give the majority of newcomers much chance.) But, I hear you say, why can't you find a publisher for yourself? You can – and I'll explain in a moment how you can – which neatly disposes of the first apparent necessity for a literary agent. Before you congratulate yourself on saving the agent's commission – currently between at least 10 and 15 per cent – let's consider the next step.

'We liked your novel/Icelandic cookery book/synopsis on the sex life of the armadillo and should like to publish/commission it,' the publisher writes. You're in! Hooray. The Booker Prize (if it's a novel), if not the Nobel, looms on the horizon. When you've finished celebrating with admiring family and friends, you return to the publisher's letter, trying to be businesslike and concentrate. The letter goes on to say: 'We can offer you an advance of . . . against royalties of . . .'

You probably know that 'royalties' are a percentage of the moneys accruing from the sale of your book and that an 'advance' is what it sounds like: a sum of money advanced to you in anticipation of future earnings. Your publisher now opens an account in your name, just like a bank manager: you start with an overdraft (except that only in quite unusual circumstances will you be asked to repay it).

Basic royalties on general hardback books start usually at 10 per cent of the selling price. They are unlikely to start higher. If they start lower, you might ask why. So far so good. But is the advance offered more or less what you expected? Happily more? Or disappointingly less? Depends what you expected. If you've been reading in the popular press of that first novel that fetched six figures you may have had grandiose ideas (you are being offered three or four). That's because the six-figure advance was news. Don't run away with the idea that it's typical. The real questions you should be asking yourself are, 'Is this offer competitive? Would another publisher offer more?' Unfortunately, this can be added to the list of things this book won't tell you (nor could anyone tell you without reading the MS and knowing which publisher you are dealing with). That's the agent's next job: evaluating the work and comparing it with other, comparable works he's negotiated with this particular publisher.

Let's pause and take stock. You are considering a firm offer from a publisher, reading his letter for the umpteenth time. The temptation simply to accept is bound to be almost overwhelming. Will you argue the toss and risk losing the deal? Because, let's face it, the deck is stacked heavily in the publisher's favour. Unless he is exceptionally keen, he is quite prepared to let your book go if you're going to be unreasonable or difficult. He has plenty of other new authors queuing up. Most authors would much prefer to take the bird in hand, rather than risk chancing their arm again elsewhere. So, to be impartial about this, would most agents. I have on more than one occasion apologized to an author for recommending acceptance of terms I don't think as good as they ought to be if they are as good as I can get; only very seldom have I recommended rejecting them. It would be a rash agent who recommended turning down a final offer of almost any sort – when he'd been unable to improve on it – unless he was confident of placing the book in question elsewhere. If he thereafter fails to place it at all, he will have egg on his face, and it's his client who is going to throw the first egg.

A competent agent will never lose a deal through a negotiation, no matter how tough. However strongly he disagrees with the publisher, he always has a line of retreat – strategic withdrawal. He can say in the end, 'I think your offer is appalling, but I will put it to my client, and he must decide.' The client may then say he thinks it's smashing and all remain friends, honour being satisfied all round. (This is because the agent, having battled, has told the author this is the best he's going to get and he may as well put a good face on it. If the author has battled, there is the risk that both sides would end up disgruntled; here both sides blame the agent for being greedy or difficult, which is fine.)

The fact is, the agent–publisher relationship goes far beyond your book. Publishing is a small world, where practically everybody who is anybody on the buying and selling sides knows everybody else. If a publisher takes a firm line and virtually obliges me to accept (on behalf of a client) poorish terms (which I accept rather than lose a deal), he knows as well as I that the next time round he will come low on my list. I'll be offering MSS in future to others with whom I know I can negotiate more reasonably before coming back to him as a last resort. This may not matter too much; but other agents are going to reach the same conclusion, and in the end, if the mean publisher winds up bottom of everybody's list, it matters a great deal. All he'll be getting from agents is MSS most of his competitors have declined. This is only part of the story, but it's the relevant part here.

This is assuming that the publisher is offering less than the going rate, where the agent can be useful if only by establishing that it can't be improved, without involving you, the author, in acrimony. But supposing the publisher's offer is fair, even generous (it doesn't happen every day, but it's possible)? I implied doubts on your saving yourself the agent's commission, and the reason was that the agent will most often cancel that out by obtaining at the very least 10 per cent more than you would have got yourself, even if the deal is unexciting. But we're looking now at an offer that is excellent. Only a foolish or short-sighted agent will invariably press for better terms for a new author, unless he's convinced it's a potential bestseller. If he makes a habit of doing so automatically, publishers will just as automatically offer him less than they are prepared to pay, allowing him his game of horse-trading and giving him the satisfaction of thinking he's won, when he probably hasn't. It's fun, and everybody enjoys it, but it doesn't get the author anywhere. We're dealing with examples that are getting more rare than common, admittedly, but still suggesting a saving of the agent's commission by dealing direct, if the agent is recommending acceptance of the publisher's original offer (which he might have made to you anyway).

Still playing the devil's advocate, let's take the next step for you, the unagented author, still 10 per cent (at least) better off than your agented contemporaries.

The publisher's contract arrives through the letterbox with a printed slip attached indicating where to initial and sign and asking you not to date it yet. It looks impressive, and you are impressed. It will be a printed document, and though some of the clauses will have space for details of royalties and percentages, most of the clauses won't. In print they will look like the laws of the Medes and Persians – unalterable. Of course you will read it. If you are one of those commendably exceptional, conscientious or pernickety people who actually read the small print at the back of a hire purchase agreement, you will read every word. If you understand it you will be even more exceptional. An experienced agent will not only understand it, he will attack the Medes and Persians with a ballpoint, crossing out here and adding bits there and sending it back for a retype. That's something else the agent does. (In fact, many agents draw up their own agreements, though some publishers still insist on using their own; or they may have an agreed compromise form for use with a particular agency.) Does it begin to look as if an agent is indispensable?

Not quite.

You can join one of the authors' trade unions, the Society of Authors or the Writers' Guild – for a fee, naturally – either of which will advise you on a publisher's contract, clause by clause. They won't advise you on the notional terms for your particular book, because they won't have read it and can't be expected to, but they will tell you if the terms in general are fair and reasonable. And, if you have no agent, this is to be recommended. Alternatively you could take your contract to a solicitor, but for reasons explained later (see Lawyers on page 166) this is probably not a good idea.

Right. You have found yourself a publisher, had his contract professionally vetted and, if necessary amended, and signed up. And you have done all this without an agent. You are an author without an agent.

Wrong. You are an author without a literary agent.

Publisher or agent? I put it like that to catch your eye, but, the truth is, it's somewhat misleading. Hereafter you are going to have an 'agent' whether you like it or not. Let me explain.

Most authors, other than certain academics and specialists writing for a limited readership, hope – at least hope – that the original publication of their book won't be the end of the story. We are now looking at exciting things called subsidiary rights. Even before publication in volume form, extracts from your book could appear in a newspaper or magazine (see Serial Rights on page 171). It could be published in the USA or in translation in any number of foreign countries. It might even be filmed for cinema or television or dramatized for the live theatre.

I don't mean to raise unrealistic hopes. Very few books indeed lend themselves to all or any of these. But lots do to at least some. And if they do, these rights need to be explored, whether sales result or not. If you have a literary agent, he will most likely sell the publisher a limited licence to publish in book form in the English language (probably excluding the USA). Other rights – the subsidiary rights – he will hang on to and endeavour to sell separately. If you have no literary agent, the publisher will normally take all rights in your book, and he will be doing precisely the same thing, very likely through the same associate literary agencies abroad. Thus the publisher is now acting as your agent, taking a 'commission' just as the literary agent does, though usually more and sometimes a great deal more. The main difference is that your share will be credited to your account (remember the overdraft?) and you won't actually see the money until your account is in credit and even then not necessarily until the next accounting period, which could mean waiting six months or in some cases a year. With an agent, you usually collect as the subsidiary cash comes in. That is the general picture; as I've warned again and again there are exceptions, and terms are infinitely variable. Certainly with some publishers the terms of their contracts with unagented authors are improving considerably. But publishers are not charities, and like any business they are bound to buy their books as competitively if not as cheaply as they can in the marketplace.

I know one author who would refute the entire last paragraph by pointing out, perfectly legitimately, that it's possible to be your own agent and negotiate subsidiary rights by yourself without giving anybody a commission percentage. But then he claims to enjoy the business side of authorship more than the actual writing bit; also he is a highly professional and experienced author, familiar with the business of negotiating and terms (he would make an excellent agent). Most of us would prefer the writing bit and leave the transactions of yen and kroner to someone else.

We've progressed a good way from the concept of the new and untried author already. But we need to look ahead a little more yet, to the established author, which is after all what you're setting out to become. What does the agent do for him?

I said earlier that the first answer to the question, 'What does and agent do?' was, 'Finds you a publisher'. But the established author already has a publisher, perhaps waiting eagerly for his next MS. The agent may read it first and perhaps make useful suggestions. He may not. He may be able to improve the terms. But again he may not, particularly if the terms for the previous book were already excellent or if the last book's sales don't justify an improvement. In effect, he may be simply playing postman and sending your new MS to the publisher, collecting his commission on the way; you could say for nothing apart from subsidiary rights, which may or may not result, depending on the nature of the book. And if that's all there is to it, loyalty apart, you are arguably better off managing on your own.

Usually, however, that isn't the whole story. The agent, remember, takes his commission on what he actually sells. It may be easily earned, in the case of established authors, in the sort of hypothetical case we've just envisaged. Not infrequently the agent will handle work for a regular client which he wouldn't touch with a barge-pole for anyone else; the very long shot, which has only a remote chance of publication, the odd article, the collection of verse which as we know stands to bring in insufficient commission to cover the cost of offering it, not to mention all those letters discussing your work and maybe even the one to your bank manager assuring him that cash is on the way.

Even so, if you write, consistently, the same type of book and have the right publisher for your work, who deals very well with subsidiary rights – and you aren't in a hurry for the cash anyway – you may be perfectly happy dealing direct. (If you suddenly write something quite different which doesn't suit your publisher's list, he may be disinclined to advise you to take it to a rival firm in case he loses you altogether.) Dealing direct is particularly appropriate for academics and specialists, where subsidiary rights may especially be relatively unimportant. In this case there may be no good reason for working through an agent.

This is necessarily a somewhat superficial run-through of the differences between the two, publisher or agent. But if it has enabled you to make up your mind, initially at least – if you deal direct you can always go to an agent later and, perhaps surprisingly, a number of authors have done – it brings us to the next decision.

Choosing a publisher

Poeta nascitur non fit, as the saying goes, and which I translate for the benefit of those with no Latin – and to the irritation of Latinists – the poet is born, not made. Lewis Carroll jocularly reversed the order – *fit non nascitur* – and he may have been right, but that's by the by. Whether writers are born writers is.debatable, but almost invariably they are born readers, as we've already noted. Tennyson is supposed to have said that the first poetry to thrill him was his own, but most writers got the bug first of all by being thrilled by someone else's books. Let's assume, then, that I'm not far wrong if I conjecture that you strongly admire the writing of some established and probably well-known author or maybe several; also that he or she is – or they are – more or less contemporary (classics and long-dead authors make for good inspiration but bad precedents). If I'm right, you're off to a flying start. If, as is highly likely, you are yourself writing something not too dissimilar, try that author's publisher. Logically the editor responsible, if he hasn't left the firm, should share your taste and, with luck, will like your book and publish it. There are a million reasons why he might do neither, but it's a good starting point anyway and well worth a try.

This approach can be extended to include those publishers who generally bring out the *sort* of books you like. When you read a book you enjoy make a note of the publisher. (Oddly, hardly anyone does. The next time someone recommends a book to you, ask who published it. Ten to one they won't have a clue.) If it's a hardback book the publisher's name will be on the spine and the title page. If it's paperback, which term, as we shall see in a moment, includes any book bound in a stiffened paper cover, it will very likely be a reprint, in which case the original, hardback publisher's name will be printed inside. If it isn't then it will be an original paperback, and it's the paperback publisher you will be interested in. Browse through bookshops. I need hardly add that the word sort is in italics above for a good reason. Clearly a publisher who has just produced a biography of Robert Browning isn't going to want another one. There are reference books that list established publishers and their preferences. *The Writer's Handbook* or the *The Writers' and Artists' Yearbook* are musts. Both reference books will, however, give the broad requirements of most publishers: those, for example, who publish no fiction or children's books at all, ever. They are especially useful if your book is in one of the specialist fields. They won't give exhaustive lists, because new publishers are springing up every day, usually small houses but often run by experienced editors.

You will, however, probably try the biggest and best-known publishers first, if only because they are the only ones you've heard of: the famous names. Fair enough. They have the money available to pay a decent advance and the organization ready and waiting for the maximum promotion and publicity you could expect. They may be absolutely right for you. On the other hand, you may not be right for them. They will already have a strong list of well-established authors and, unless they see your book as a 'lead title' – those that head their main lists and get the lion's share of promotion, usually strongly commercial books – or just possibly of an unusually fine literary quality in line for one of the prestigious prizes, they may well decline. They will have an abundance of new authors clamouring at their doors and, with the best will in the world, can take only a minute percentage. I recall selling what I considered an outstanding first novel to the head of one of the biggest publishing houses over lunch (not really; nobody reads MSS between the soup and the savoury, but we discussed it) but was dismayed later, when their list of forthcoming titles was circulated, to see my author in the middle of what looked like a page from the London telephone directory. Surely they could have done better than this! Then I looked at the list again. My author was sandwiched between some of the best-known names in publishing. A small fish in a very large pond.

So how about being a large fish in a small pond? If yours is one of the lead titles on a small list, you may do better than by being an also-ran on a vast one. Swings and roundabouts. If yours is, again, a specialist book, there is a good case for going to a smaller, specialist publisher who knows his market better than anybody. Small publishers, lacking the resources to cover the whole range even if they wanted to, do tend to specialize and can do very well in their more limited field.

It is a mistake, in any case, to think of small publishers as 'second best', in the sense that they are more likely to take you than the big boys are. True, they are more likely to be on the lookout for promising authors, even if they're not yet too commercial. But against that is the fact that they can less well afford to take risks with their limited budgets and write off disasters against the assured earners who provide their bread and butter and sometimes cake.

In the end, your target is the publisher who appears to be of like mind to yourself. In many categories that's no problem: if you write science fiction, look around and see which publishers are most successful with this particular genre. Apply this to any category. 'General' books are more difficult to pinpoint, but much the same rule applies. The one who publishes books you like is, in all probability, the right one.

Paperback

As we have seen, a paperback is any book bound in a stiffened paper cover, as opposed to hardbacks bound in cloth – though these days it's more usually embossed paper made to look like cloth. There are broadly two different kinds of paperbacks, but as most people think of 'paperbacks' as those little books seen everywhere on bookstalls and in newsagents and supermarkets – those which the trade calls 'mass market' – let's consider them first.

Since paperbacks are cheaper than hardbacks, it will come as no surprise to learn that those are far and away the main sales for popular novelists and authors of certain types of popular non-fiction.

Before you pick me up for using 'popular' twice in one sentence, let me say that it wasn't accidental. Popular is the key word. I have to generalize here, but as a very rough guide let's say that a fairly typical hardback book with nothing remarkable going for it will cover its production costs after a sale of between 1,000 and 1,500 copies, depending on the quality of paper, the print run and cover price. For a mass-market paperback the break-even figure could be anywhere between 10,000 and 20,000.

I did say a hardback book with nothing remarkable going for it. Naturally, if it is earmarked for stardom, and has justified a high advance, these figures could go through the roof. But the comparison stands. Hence a worthy book of somewhat limited appeal to a less-than-mass readership is unlikely to qualify for paperback. To put it crudely, unless a book has other claims to public attention – if, say, it won the Booker Prize – the tendency is downmarket; definitely the lower slopes of Parnassus. (The same is true of the television programmes that have the highest ratings.)

So if yours is a novel of literary quality, but not the stuff lots of people are going to get excited about, don't be disappointed if it never 'goes into paperback'. Many of the best books never do.

When your book is accepted by a hardback publisher, he will, if he thinks there's a chance, do his best to arrange with another publisher for a paperback reprint to follow his own publication, to appear up to twelve months later, probably sooner these days, by which time his own hardback sales will have declined or ceased, so the cheap version won't kill it. As he will, if it's sold to a separate house, collect up to 50 per cent of the proceeds (see Agreements on page 153) he will probably try quite hard.

This is assuming that paperbacks are reprints of hardback books and that there are hardback and paperback publishing houses and never the twain shall meet: neither of which is true.

Some publishers certainly issue hardback editions only, or at least don't publish for the mass-market, but more and more of the bigger houses now have their own paperback lists within the firm, though under a different imprint. If that's the case, they may elect to publish the paperback reprint themselves. If they do, in most cases all the paperback income will go to the author; you don't usually stand to lose a percentage at all. This looks attractive and may well be. The other side of that particular coin is that you may not have the benefit of a separate advance for the paperback; if the book is really commercial, an outside paperback house will pay far more than an inside one, especially if an auction is involved, with several houses bidding. Your own publisher's paperback side isn't going to bid against itself.

Also, these days it has become increasingly common for the paperback houses to initiate publication; to take on a book as an 'original' paperback, with no hardback involved at all. If the book you liked acknowledges no hardback original, try that house direct. This used to apply almost exclusively to non-fiction, in popularly priced series appealing to, again, a fairly wide readership not prepared or able to pay hardback prices; students, for example. Nowadays there is a marked increase in original paperback popular fiction.

Just as the original hardback publisher controls paperback rights, so the original paperback publisher will normally control hardback rights. He may lease these on your behalf, in what is aptly called a 'reverse deal'. This doesn't happen too often and when it does it is more likely to be with works of non-fiction than fiction, though, again, some hardback publishers have used the reverse deal to build up a fiction list of well-established authors quickly, which can be especially valuable for new publishers. And, naturally, this is helpful to the authors, too, especially as their share of the deal will be something like 80 per cent instead of as low as 50 per cent on the hardcover-to-paperback sub-lease. Before you get too excited, I should explain that the hardback deal, buying from paperback, is unlikely to be very remunerative, since the rights are limited: the hardback publisher is of course denied the usual cut of paperback rights. Nor is he likely to sell huge numbers of copies if – as may happen – the paperback has already been published; but he will be able to supply libraries and book clubs and those who prefer to buy books they want to keep.

The other kind of paperback is known by various names in the trade, but perhaps the most common is 'trade paperback', as copies are sold through trade outlets – bookshops and bookstalls – rather than through supermarkets and the like. They are generally identical copies of the original edition but bound in paper instead of hardback and therefore come in all shapes and sizes, but may be 'original' in the sense that they are the only edition published, yet still in a conventional format. Their anticipated sale may be around 5,000 copies rather than 10,000, though some publishers would put the figure higher. They will, as you'd expect, be cheaper than hardback but considerably more expensive than mass-market books. It isn't unusual for them to be produced simultaneously with a hardback edition – especially if they are reference books.

Packagers
These aren't strictly publishers, though some do publish, but mainly firms, great and small, which do everything a publisher does except publish. Their expertise lies in the field of design and production, and for this reason they mainly confine themselves to well-illustrated books where these factors are important and complicated. The result of their labours – the printed book – is then sold to a publisher, who in turn sells it through the trade to the public, naturally for a good deal more than he paid for it. Most of the time, of course, publishers design and produce their own

books. Sometimes, if the design aspect is vital, and the publisher's own resources can't conveniently cope, he may farm it out to a packager. If this is the case, then it doesn't concern you, the author, in the least.

Often, though, it is the packager himself who initiated the whole thing. He produces the basic idea for a book – probably dozens; but only a few will work out – and finds a suitably qualified author for it, often by canvassing agents. Author and packager will then thrash out an outline and the author will prepare a brief sample, or specimen of the text, for which he will normally – but not always, if he's prepared to take a chance – be paid a fee. The packager will add some specimen illustrations or artwork, combining this to produce a dummy – a mock-up of the book consisting of a few pages more or less as they will appear in the final version, and a lot of blank ones – and probably a colourful jacket. Armed with this he will approach publishers, overseas as well as at home, and invite them to give firm orders for copies. If he doesn't get sufficient orders, he will have to abandon the project and start something else. How does all this affect you, the nominated author?

If the project falls on its face for lack of support, you should retain the basic fee for the work you've done, and anything you've actually written should be returned to you. *Finis*. If the book does go ahead, then you will have an agreement, the terms of which will have been worked out at the start, rather as if you were dealing with a publisher direct. The terms, however, will be very different. Your remuneration, in relation to the number of copies sold, will be appreciably less, because it will be based – whether royalty or fee – not on the retail price of the book but on the price the packager receives from the publisher for the copies. If it's a fee, or lump sum, then provision should be made for further sums, pro rata, if more copies are sold from further printings than were originally anticipated. But, whether fees or royalties, you stand to get a lot less than you would be entitled to expect from a comparable publishing contract. However, the chances are that you wouldn't *get* a comparable contract from a publisher. A packager will go ahead only if the number of copies he knows he can dispose of is considerable – hopefully including overseas publishers, too – most probably many, many more than a publisher on his own would risk printing. A small percentage on a huge number is better than a large percentage on a small one. And you stand to collect your cash 'up front' without waiting for those half-yearly or annual statements to limp in. The packager pays you on copies sold, in bulk, to the publishers. Whether they are thereafter sold to the public matters not at all. (Of course it does; but it doesn't affect your remuneration, unless more copies are ordered.) It can also introduce the author's name to a much wider public than he could expect on a normal deal.

There are editorial packagers who neither design nor produce books but do produce ideas and authors, generally editing the result for publishers. These are often composite books with a number of contributors. If you are involved with them, you will be paid outright as a rule, though you may come in for a share of royalties if not too many contributors are involved.

Vanity publishing

This is the derogatory term for having a book published at the author's expense, it being presumed (or proved) that no regular, commercial publisher will take it on, either because it isn't good enough or because its sales potential looks unpromising. So you try a publisher who requests a subsidy, or in some cases the full cost of production, followed by an inflated royalty which would make your fortune in the unlikely event that large sales result. You will get a glowing report from the publisher's reader recommending publication. (I don't know if they are always glowing, but the only ones I've seen have invariably been.) The snag is that the true vanity publisher lacks any real means of distribution. He may advertise to a limited extent with little or no facilities for getting copies into bookshops, which would mean a team of reps touring the countryside. In which case you would do better to go direct to a printer and have him deliver finished copies to your doorstep. Anyone can be his or her own publisher, and you then dispose of copies as best you can. This has certainly been done successfully, though not often.

That's the worst scenario.

It should be said, though, that there are nowadays 'vanity' publishers who strongly resent the term: those who request a very much more modest investment on a profit-sharing basis which can – and to my knowledge has – produced a genuine profit. Sometimes they will waive the contribution altogether if they have sufficient faith in the work. What to look for is the actual amount of cash they are calling for. Risk as much as you can comfortably afford to lose – and quite probably will if we are looking at thousands.

If your aim is higher, you could try a general publisher with the suggestion that you pay for the cost of production or part of it. Most publishers wouldn't want to know, but there are several who might, again on the basis that once the initial productions costs had been recovered you would get a much higher than normal royalty, the publisher taking a percentage for his distribution costs, overheads and a modest profit. He won't do this in any case unless your book is one that won't disgrace his list. The chances of exciting sales are still remote, but at least your book will be fairly widely offered, and no one except you and the publisher will know that vanity comes into it.

As ever, there have been some magnificent exceptions: authors who have published their books themselves and sold thousands of copies, which the general publishers they tried never considered possible.

Internet publishing

The e-revolution in publishing is developing so fast that it one can only speculate as to the future, but at present it looks a bit like the curate's egg. Some e-publishers have sprung up offering publication only on the Internet (usually for a specified period before rights revert to the author), others are co-publishing with traditional publishers in both formats. Some are vanity publishers in disguise while there are much more reputable outfits who seek to publish only quality material that, for whatever reason, hasn't found a home elsewhere. In fact, one e-book was officially accepted as an entry for the Booker Prize in 1998, proving that it is a medium that should not be discounted.

The Internet's value for publishers who advertise and promote traditional books online is beyond doubt, and unpublished authors can offer a 'teaser', even a sample chapter, with the hope of attracting sufficient numbers of punters to encourage traditional publication.

Publishing a book in its entirety on the Internet is one method. Another, to get people hooked, is to publish in chapters or sections. The risks in this form of publishing are that the cost of setting the site up and advertising could exceed the profit, the fact that a buyer can make unlimited copies of a piece once downloaded and that the numbers calling for the next episode of a title published in sections might dwindle.

To date Stephen King is the highest-profile writer to publish in this medium, and chapters of his novel *The Plant* were made available to download for a fee. The initial interest suggested that this was to be a great success, but it wasn't sustained, intimating that novelty value was a prime motivator. The drop in interest prompted King to discontinue the run – though by doing this an author could be sued for breach of contract with ongoing subscribers. However, despite potential pitfalls, at the time of writing at least two other major writers, Frederick Forsyth and Fay

Weldon, are promising to publish work in this way, though the bestselling science fantasy writer Terry Pratchett has said that he won't.

Even though there may be perceived advantages to a reader accessing a work in this way, I doubt if many people would be satisfied with ending up in bed with 200 pages of loose-leaf A4 rather than a bound book. There is an alternative, true: Casio's hand-held mini-computer works like a book, with 'pages' that can be 'turned'. Something better may be invented in the future, but, though I may be proved wrong, I strongly suggest that keen readers of books will be reluctant to relinquish the pleasure of browsing through a bookshop's wide range of titles for the inspiration of serendipity, turning the pages by hand and, yes, even the smell of a volume that needs no batteries and looks good on the shelf. If I am wrong, traditional publishers, already in danger of losing some leading authors to the e-book, might disappear altogether. Now there's a thought.

In truth, the probable outcome will be a combination of traditional and e-publishing. Certain types of book, perhaps with a limited or specialist appeal and which don't need to be beautiful objects – technical manuals, for instance – would lend themselves well to the new technology. Full-colour art books or coffee-table items, until such time as home-printer technology and speed of download time have advanced considerably, are likely to remain the province of those that know how to do it best: the traditional publisher.

Choosing an agent

This can be more difficult because you can't browse through the bookshops and see who agented what. Agents don't advertise, for practical rather than ethical reasons: nobody wants a flood of bottom drawer MSS, long abandoned, which need some consideration, letters and the business of returning them to their owners.

The best bet is personal recommendation. Sometimes a kindly publisher will suggest one, or several, if your book isn't right for his list but looks not unpromising. Another author will usually recommend his own agent if he has one. Failing that, you have to fall back on the reference books. *The Writer's Handbook*, at the time I'm writing this, lists 149 UK literary agents, and this list isn't exhaustive. It is limited to established and recognized agencies; in recent years the business has proliferated, drawing in some able ex-publishers and editors. There are no formal qualifications: anybody can be an agent or act as one. Hence agencies may be individuals working alone. They may be companies with a comparatively large staff. They may be old-established firms with highly distinguished contemporary names on their list – and even more distinguished dead ones if their work is still in copyright. You may even have heard of one or two.

Once again, the trade publications will give you a clue. But, as with publishers, though many agencies will helpfully announce what they don't want – often short pieces, short stories, articles and verse – they are shy of admitting what they are best and worst at. They may deal mainly with play scripts but won't discourage you from sending along a novel just in case it's a hot one. They may specialize in book rights but will accept scripts, especially if there's a good book in the offing. In fact most agencies, unless they specify otherwise, will consider book-length MSS for adults and children, films and plays and will deal with all rights arising from them. Those who specialize in a limited field, such as children's books, and say so aren't necessarily the best at it, but they are probably good and know the market as well as anybody and better than most. If your MS looks right for one of these, try them.

Otherwise, before you take a pin and stick it somewhere in the pages listing 149, ask yourself what sort of agent you would prefer.

Big or small, for instance.

Small, as we all know, is beautiful. But big has its advantages too, and I have at this stage to allow for the indignation of the largest agencies, who could well take umbrage at my saying a moment ago that agencies won't admit what they are worst at. They would say they are good at everything. This is because they have horses for courses: separate departments which themselves specialize in handling volume, serial, translation and dramatic rights, for instance. So if your book is made into a film or a play, they will have specialists within the firm to look after these things. Smaller agencies may not have the staff to cope 'in house', that is to say, from their own office. It is virtually impossible for any one individual agent to keep abreast of developments in all the various fields or to maintain personal contact with, say, book and magazine editors, television and film producers or drama departments together with the numerous overseas connections needful for the maximum exploitation of the work handled.

Does this mean that if you're with a small book agency and television, stage or film rights crop up you're sunk? Not at all. They will pass the negotiations to another associate agency, which deals all the time with films and television and will handle these rights on their behalf. The commission will be the same, split between the two agencies. In the end it comes to much the same thing.

You have one personal, main 'agent' – the one you complain to when things go wrong. Whether rights are passed on to someone else within the agency or to an outside associate shouldn't make any difference. When it comes to selling rights overseas, all agencies work through foreign associates, the only exception being that some deal direct with the USA – and most do sometimes. If you feel happier with all your work under one roof, so to speak, a bigger agency may suit you better. If you prefer to deal with one person with a perhaps closer grasp on all aspects of your work, the smaller one may be right for you. Again, you could be a bigger fish in a smaller pond.

As with publishers, the bigger the agency, the stronger their list will be, including some well-known bestsellers and distinguished authors. The smaller agencies will have fewer; if they accumulated too many they would become big themselves and some, like some publishers, don't want to. Again, big will, or should, have an efficient administration and skilled and experienced negotiators – though as a first-time author you are likely to be allotted a junior member, who may be less skilled but perhaps a bit more enthusiastic. If your book isn't obviously a potential bestseller, they may not want you: I have had would-be novelists who approached me tentatively, saying up to six agencies had declined even to consider a first novel. In the end, as with publishers – there is a lot of common ground – your aim is to find the agent who will best represent your work; which generally means the one most sympathetic to it.

10 The approach

Having made your choice between publisher and agent, you are now, so to speak, well down the fairway, having avoided – if you've been following me – at least the worst of the bunkers and, with your eye firmly on the flag, you are ready for the approach shot. What's the best way of going about it?

Publishers don't always offer advice on this, though some do. Quite a few agents make it known that they require, or at least prefer, a preliminary letter. In general, with agents and publishers this is always a good idea. To clear the ground, let's dispose of those instances when it isn't.

Those publishers who tell you they will consider only MSS submitted by literary agencies will hate me for this, but while I'm all for encouraging them in pursuing this course, I don't actually believe that if a MS lands on their desk they won't at least glance at it before sending it winging back or hang on to it if it looks highly promising.

Best send a covering letter with a précis and not more than a dozen pages of sample text along with an stamped addressed envelope or an International Reply Coupon. If it's necessary to go into much personal detail, it's probably better to attach this separately in the form of a curriculum vitae; but only if it's genuinely helpful. With a full MS never, never write a long letter explaining your book. The eventual buyer isn't going to read it, and the book must explain itself. If you have to explain it, you are saying in effect that it needs explaining. Some novelists do include a page or so with a précis of the story – helpful if not too long – though it can be useful for non-fiction, in which case it may appear in the printed book itself in the form of an extended contents list.

If your book is very much off-beat (non-category), it will be difficult or impossible for the publisher to form an opinion without reading it and, since you won't be able to explain it in a preliminary letter, skip it, break the rule and send the MS.

It isn't a bad idea to find out the name of the editor on whose desk letter or MS will land and address it to him or her. A quick telephone call will elicit this information. All you have to do is to say, 'I am sending you the manuscript of a novel/book on dressage/book for young (or older) children/history of Tongoland . . . Could you let me know whom I should address it to?' A small firm will tell you; the answer could even be 'Me'. So will (or should) the operator on the switchboard of a big firm. Not only does the subsequent submission create a good impression on the recipient – you are clearly a professional who isn't sending out stuff just anywhere; he or she won't know about the preliminary enquiry – it also means you have an immediate contact in case you need to chase up (which we'll come to). It may be a small point, but a writer who takes trouble in one direction will take trouble all along the line, and a letter addressed to a named individual is more likely to be taken seriously than the 'Dear Sir or Madam' type.

Agents usually list the members of the firm in trade directories, so the problem shouldn't arise; publishers, if they list names at all, frequently give only the directors, which your eventual editor may not be. I said agents should be sent a preliminary letter, but if your enquiry is a straightforward and simple one, such as 'Are you willing to consider a first novel?', a brief telephone call may suffice. (As we noted, some agencies will say no.)

On receiving a MS, the publisher or agent should acknowledge receipt by letter or postcard. If he doesn't within a reasonable time you can drop him a line or telephone (his secretary preferably) just to confirm that it arrived safely. Don't take the line that because they haven't immediately written back they don't care. Assume the generous best, not the worst – there are plenty of valid reasons for the deafening silence: perhaps he is actually reading it and will write as soon as he's finished (see Complaints on page 199).

If it's a full-length MS, allow a month as minimum for the agent's or publisher's decision; longer if it's an abstruse subject, which may have to be sent to an outside reader for an expert opinion. You may of course get a reaction within days, either because they are over the moon about it or because they dismissed it as hopeless on the strength of the first dozen pages. As someone (I wish I could remember who) once said, 'You don't need to eat a whole meal to know whether you like it or not.'

If you're one of those unfortunate but not uncommon people whose stomach ties itself in knots every time the postman calls, waiting can be agony. Maybe a month isn't too bad (at least you haven't been rejected out of hand); but if six publishers decline that's six months at least. Probably much more (I've actually known publishers take up to twelve months over a marginal book, believe it or not). Can we not speed up the process?

Certainly. The author can give a deadline. Unless the publisher (or agent, though agents are rarely too slow) comes up with a decision within, say, the next fortnight, the author will withdraw the book. Fine. That means that if the publisher can't quite make up his mind, he isn't totally committed; and if he isn't totally committed, you have made up his mind for him. Back comes your MS. Which is, of course, why occasionally publishers are allowed to take their time, however long – while there is still a real chance that they will accept.

Very well, then; we don't want to lose a reasonable chance. But can't we, if we can afford it, have six or even a dozen copies of letters or even our MS made and send them out in all directions at once?

Yes, but.

Some authors do just that. So do agents. It will certainly save time in reaching a conclusion on whether your book is acceptable or not. It will also be expensive with MSS. Extra photocopies will cost you a small fortune as will paper and ink if you run them off a computer; if you have no agent you can add massive postage. It would cost the agent the same, plus the time taken off other work. Hence agents are somewhat disinclined to go in for multiple submissions, as we call it, unless they are pretty sure they are on to a good thing, though it is more common than it used to be. But even if the expense is, as they say, no object, there are other considerations.

Ethics come into it. As a newcomer you can pretend to be ignorant of the customs of the book trade (which an agent can't), but I don't advise it. If a publisher is seriously interested in your book he will have it read, quite possibly by an outside reader, to whom he will be paying a fee (plus postage again). He may have several reports and, if they are encouraging, he may read it himself; in a small house he may read it himself and make his decision right away. Even then, he has to consider how many copies he estimates it's safe to print and, from this, depending on the length of the book, what he would need to price it at, taking into account the printing and paper costs, of course, and overheads. When he has done all this, he will be in a position to make an offer. If you then tell him you're sorry, but in the meantime you have sold the book to someone else, he will be not too pleased (and you will go on his hit list). If you were an agent, he would be furious and quite rightly.

If the agent is offering a MS simultaneously to more than one publisher – which usually means he is auctioning it to see who will be the highest bidder – he will make this plain to all concerned. If he doesn't, the publisher is entitled to assume that he has the exclusive offer and that if he makes a reasonable offer it will, subject to haggling perhaps, be accepted. Sometimes a publisher, invited to join in an auction, will decline to do so. In any case, he should be given the opportunity. But auctions are not too common. Few MSS lend themselves to this kind of treatment.

It would be rare and probably unwise for an author to offer a MS to more than one agent at a time, if only because if more than one agreed to take it on he would be stuck: they are not going to compete in terms of commission and will be cross if he's wasted their time.

A publisher will appreciate and may indeed insist on your including return postage with your MS, in case he has to send it back; an agent will insist on it. This is one reason why, if you're trying an agent, a preliminary letter is best. Another is that some agents will charge you a modest reading or 'consideration' fee in addition to the postage. This used to be considered rather disreputable; I've never understood why, since reading a manuscript takes up the time of professional people, which itself has to be paid for one way or another, even if the answer is a straight rejection. But the placing of MSS with publishers has become more and more difficult and the number of would-be authors has not declined, which equals an ever-increasing number of unsaleable MSS on the agent's desk. If the agent is to justify the time these take to turn round, he may require a fee towards his overheads – it will seldom cover them. Another reason is that it discourages some writers from sending in one unsaleable MS after another, despite off-putting rejections, which can happen, and does.

There are still agents who don't charge and, if the idea of fees worries you, go to them. One reason they may not charge anything is that, if they do, they owe you a reader's report on the work. They might well feel obliged to give at least some reasons for declining. If they haven't charged you anything, you can't grumble if their rejection simply consists of 'No thank you'.

Working relationships

Whether you are dealing with an agent or a publisher direct, there are simple guidelines which, if followed, will smooth the path to a successful and amicable working relationship. Perhaps the simplest run-through of this relationship is to cover it in terms of Do's and Don'ts.

DO, if it's an agent you're approaching, write a preliminary letter to find out if he is interested in principle in taking you on. A stamped addressed envelope is obligatory, not so much to save expense but to save time. He may have a full list or may not deal with the type of book you're offering. As I've explained, a telephone call may suffice if the enquiry is a straightforward one. But if you telephone, be brief. It's unlikely that he or she is sitting at the other end of the telephone with nothing else to do. With a publisher, it's not necessary for fiction – if you've chosen a suitable one – but still a good idea for non-fiction: he may have something similar already on the stocks or feel your subject isn't right for his list. This saves time all round.

DON'T seek a preliminary meeting until agent or editor has had a chance to read something of your work. Talking about it is usually a waste of everybody's time – yours and theirs. I have so often found that I got on well with a would-be author and liked him or her, only to discover when they'd done that their written work was something I couldn't take on, which is embarrassing and unhelpful. Publishers have the same experience. It's different if you are asked to call, and you will be if the project is viable, and a discussion would be helpful. But wait to be invited. However, you may be excused in any case if you live a long way away and are in the area for only a day or two.

DON'T submit untidy, heavily corrected, generally scruffy or badly packaged MSS unless you don't care what impression you are making.

DON'T, if you are a newish author, telephone for news when a letter or postcard would do as well. Especially, don't be surprised if, when all you've given on the telephone is your name and the question: 'Any news of my book?', you get an evasive answer. Given a breather, your agent or publisher will unscramble his mental pigeon holes and come up with the answer. I knew one agent who could tell you offhand which publisher was currently considering any one of the multitude of books his firm was handling; but such prodigies are rare, and I am not one of them. I often have to reach for the card index. I also find it impossible to carry in my head the plots or themes of up to a hundred MSS. Mostly the title – which you omitted to give – will recall it; even the most cursory glance at the MS itself will bring it back. This doesn't mean the book is, to me, forgettable; it may be a favourite. Also I may look after more than one 'Johnson' or 'Brown'. I well remember in another agency when the late Howard Spring telephoned with a query and was mildly – but not excessively; he was a kindly man – puzzled when the switchboard appeared ignorant. He had given his name as 'Mr Spring'.

DON'T offer your book to more than one publisher at a time without making it clear that this is what you are doing; nor, if your agent is offering your book, approach a publisher yourself at the same time. Publishers will assume they have the exclusive offer otherwise, and agents' agreements with their clients – whether written or verbal, both legally binding – invariably allow them the exclusive handling of your work. You can vary the rules if you want to; but make it clear before you get involved.

DON'T, if you have an agent, discuss terms or money with the publisher. Tell him you leave all that to your agent; most publishers will assume this to be the case. This leaves you free to discuss the book itself on an amicable basis without the sordid introduction of the topic of cash. If you've indicated that you'd be happy with a low figure, your agent is going to have an uphill task persuading the publisher that a reasonable price would be five or six figures. Normally finance and terms are settled before you meet your publisher but not invariably.

DON'T sit on grievances (see Complaints on page 199). You're bound to have niggles. So is he. Air them.

DO be reasonable, especially with your agent. A time-and-motion expert investigating the working of a literary agency would probably have a fit. Properly speaking, the amount of time your agent devotes to you ought to bear some relation to the amount he earns in commission. It seldom works like that. What happens is that the most successful of his clients subsidize the others. This is true of publishers, too. But all agents and not a few publishers have at least one client who bombards them almost daily with letters or telephone calls which aren't necessary, let alone reasonable (nobody minds if they are). Try not to be one of them.

DO maintain contact, especially with your agent. Your publisher will, or should, keep you in touch with the progress of your book when it's on the way to publication, but if your agent is anything like me he will be disinclined to write to tell you that your MS has been declined by publishers A, B and C and is now with D, when that's all he has to say. He should report back periodically, but it's human nature to hang on a bit longer because there could be some good news in the offing. If you don't hear after a reasonable time, drop him a line. You will know already that this won't produce good news, but it will bring you up to date.

DO pass on any enquiries you receive about rights direct to your agent, if you have one, or to your publisher if you don't. You may be under an obligation to do so anyway.

DO discuss your overall writing plans with the agent. Make sure he knows of your especial interests or any areas in which you have expertise. This is especially important with an agent, who may be able to marry you to a publisher looking for someone like you. Agents are often the first to know of publishers who are looking for authors for specific subjects, and you may be just the one.

Of course, all this applies mainly to the newly formed relationships between author and publisher or agent. Once established, the picture may change considerably. Some authors like to keep things on a strictly business level. Others become friends with agent or editor – and even marry them! – and the business becomes more informal and relaxed, books being pretty personal things anyway. An agency in particular is, though a business, a very odd one. Like many other agents, I've sometimes had more fun selling a first novel on the eleventh offer for a modest advance than in negotiating a highly remunerative deal with a willing buyer first time out – though this can be enjoyable too.

It might seem superfluous to say – though I'm far from the first to say it – that it's less than fair or ethical to drop the agent or publisher who has taken a great deal of trouble to launch you when you were an unknown once you become established; especially unfair to leave the publisher who first took you on in favour of another who now offers possibly exaggerated terms – high advances look attractive but have to be earned in the long run. There may of course be good and valid reasons for a change; but caprice isn't one of them. You will appreciate – if and, indeed, when it applies to you – that it is seldom easy for new and untried authors to find an agent or publisher to take a chance on them. You need them more than they need you. When you are successful, the boot is on the other foot. Virtually any publisher or agent will willingly take over authors whose sales by now are guaranteed to bring in a healthy profit; reaping, that is to say, where they have not sown. Agents and publishers naturally gain as well as lose on fickle authors, benefiting from others' spade-work as well as losing on their own. But the loss of the 'gift of gratitude' is a sad one, on both sides.

Stage 4
It's Been Accepted

11 Legal

You might have been thinking that once your book is written and accepted by a publisher – allowing for discussions on, and very likely amendments to, the text – that's the end of the story in so far as you, the author, are concerned. You can sit back and relax.

That's you wearing your author's hat. Only you will find you now have two hats: author's and business person's. If you have a good agent, you have the option of planting the second firmly on his or her head and concentrating on your next *opus*. Otherwise you will need to devote some time to familiarizing yourself with the other side of publishing – the business end. Even if you have an agent, it's highly desirable to have some working knowledge of it, and the first hurdle will be the legal one.

Agreements

The possible variations in publishing agreements are pretty well endless, and no rule of thumb can be suggested for the main financial terms, which are naturally going to depend on the nature of the work (books aren't called books in agreements, they are called 'works'), the standing of the author (previous sales, celebrity value?) and the number of copies the publisher thinks, or can be persuaded to think, he can dispose of (not just his own edition, but book clubs and similar spin-offs as well), plus what rights he controls and can use to recoup his costs (paperback, serial or translation). The Society of Authors and the Writers' Guild have devised an elaborate minimum terms agreement which a limited number of publishers have accepted but, wisely I think, this deals with percentages, not with specific sums. There have been moves to try to insist on a minimum cash advance, but I think myself this would be a mistake; it could result in a new author's work being declined, when a lesser advance might have been acceptable to him – some authors have been known to settle for no advance at all in order to get a book into print, and in certain circumstances this isn't as silly as it sounds. After all, the author can always refuse an unsatisfactory offer.

Ultimately, of course, all aspects of agreements are concerned with finance in one way or another, and, if I can't offer any rules, I can at least suggest guidelines – what to look for – and perhaps clear up some common misconceptions. Let's start when the first-time author catches the postman at the door and rushes in sweeping aside the marmalade to wave a letter at his beloved, bursting out with: 'I've sold my book to Rosencrantz and Guildenstern!'

Not if he's wise he hasn't. Booksellers sell books. Authors sell rights. In fact, unless they are unwise enough to part with copyright, they don't even sell rights, they lease them. Think of your book as a house you own and the publisher as a tenant. He may rent the whole house or he may rent only a part of it. The freehold remains yours. When the tenant's lease runs out, whatever rights he had revert to you. The house is entirely at your disposal again. In the meantime all you have leased to him is the exclusive use of his part; you have undertaken not to lease it to anyone else.

A publishing agreement, like any other written agreement, is a legal document, enforceable by law. (To be pedantic, it isn't; it's a memorandum setting down what has already been agreed. Verbal agreements are equally binding, but difficult to prove.) Unlike most legal agreements or contracts, however, a considerable degree of common sense is implied rather than stated. For example, agreements very seldom specify the number of copies the publisher undertakes to print – some may do, but it's not the general practice. I once had an author, who was also a barrister, complain that there was nothing in his agreement to prevent the publisher from printing one copy of the book, thereby fulfilling his obligation to 'publish' it. But it doesn't need a legal expert to work out that this would cost the publisher a good deal of money with no way of recovering it. The publisher is every bit as keen to make money out of your book as you are. You are allies, not enemies. We have to assume that this is a partnership, a joint venture. Our concern is to see that the division of the spoils is equitable.

The first clause you will probably turn to – somewhere in the middle of the agreement – is the Advance Clause, which states how much cash you will be getting 'up front'. You will have agreed on a sum beforehand, so it won't come as a surprise. It won't, however, be paid over all at once: you will get half on signing the agreement and half on publication; or if the book is not yet written (that is, commissioned), probably a third on signature, a third on delivery of the complete MS and a third on publication. This advance should be non-returnable; that is, provided you fulfil your part of the agreement under no circumstances should you be asked to repay it. For commissioned works, this is closely linked to the Delivery Clause, which we'll come to in a moment. But let's go back and glance through a fairly typical agreement from page one.

Following the preamble which gives your name and address (the address will be your agent's if you have one) and those of your publisher, successors and assigns (you can assign your rights later to someone else if you like; the publisher may be taken over and assign his interest, though you may insist on a clause in your contract requiring your approval), is the all-important Territory Clause. This says how much of your house is to be occupied by the tenant-publisher: all of it (world rights) or only the first floor (the UK and traditional British Commonwealth and ex-Commonwealth markets, often nowadays appended in a Schedule listing all manner of islands you've never heard of) because you have – or more probably your agent has – plans for letting the other floors to separate tenants. Most unagented authors will sensibly settle for world rights – the whole shooting match – letting the publisher handle everything, including translation rights. If the publisher is limited to the UK and Commonwealth, there will usually be an addition, called the 'open market', which refers to areas in which both you and the publisher are both entitled to sell copies; generally referring to English-language copies in odd places outside the Schedule in which you – in effect usually your US publisher – and the British publisher are free to compete.

There could be complications, but generally you needn't worry too much about this clause because, if you are unagented, 'world rights', as we've seen, is appropriate for most authors; and if you have an agent he will do the worrying for you. So far, we are talking about volume rights, that is, the right to publish in book form.

Then comes the important Delivery Clause, if the work isn't yet written. If it is, a clause here will simply confirm that the publisher will publish: it should specify within a given time (between nine and twenty-four months, depending on the nature of the work and the complications in producing it if, for example, it involves design and illustrations; twelve months should be ample for a novel). The time lag may look excessive. Surely it doesn't take so long to have a book printed. Probably not. But in the first place the publisher will have to fit it into a planned schedule, among many other titles, and consider the best period in which to launch it for the maximum effect. Then he needs to have finished copies delivered from the printer well ahead of the official publication date to get copies out to potential reviewers. Finally he will need to deliver copies to booksellers who have ordered them and must have them actually in their shops on publication day. On rare occasions books have been produced and published within a matter of weeks from the delivery of the MS; but there needs to be an overriding justification for ignoring these considerations, such as highly topical subject matter.

For commissioned books this clause gives the date by which you have undertaken to hand over the completed typescript of your book, perhaps including illustrations suitable for reproduction (see Pictures and Illustrations on page 112). It could apply to the delivery of a revised MS, if the publisher has accepted on condition that you make certain changes. Allow yourself ample time if you can. Some publishers may even have a penalty clause for late delivery, and in theory it could be justification for cancelling the contract altogether, especially if the book is highly topical. In practice authors are often late in delivering the goods, and most publishers are tolerant. But if you're running late, give your publisher plenty of warning so that he can adjust schedules which have been planned many months ahead. Don't leave it until the last minute.

And here is a warning. For commissioned works, many publishers will add that the completed MS must be acceptable. Well, that sounds reasonable. You get on well with your editor, and, if he hadn't been satisfied that the end result would be acceptable, he wouldn't have commissioned it in the first place. If you make a hash of it, that's your own fault. Nobody can expect a publisher to publish a book that would be a total embarrassment on his list.

True. If you produce something unpublishable, no one should be compelled to publish it.

Only 'acceptable' doesn't equal 'publishable', and 'unacceptable' isn't the same as 'unpublishable'. Publishers reject publishable MSS every day of the week if the MSS don't happen to be suitable for their own particular lists. Since you signed your agreement, your publisher may have changed direction; that nice, enthusiastic editor may have left the firm, and his successor may not care for your book at all. On the basis of 'acceptable' he may decide that it isn't. Not to him, anyway. It's as simple as that: he doesn't choose to accept it. If, when drawing up the agreement, your publisher insists on 'acceptable', insist yourself on adding the words 'such acceptance not to be unreasonably withheld'. He can hardly resist this. There are other ways of dealing with this potential trap, and your agent may have a better one, but that's the minimum you should agree to.

If it comes to the crunch and really hinges on whether or not your final MS is publishable – or along the lines you've agreed to write it – you fall back on arbitration. Agreements sometimes have an Arbitration Clause, allowing for reference to an impartial third party. Which is as fair as you can get. A respected agent – yours – may fulfil this function. Though he is on your side, he has his professional reputation to consider, and if you're wrong it will be his sad duty to tell you so. Gently.

The Accountancy Clause will tell you how often your publishers will tot up the number of copies of your book he has sold over the previous accounting period and when you can expect to be paid. The two dates won't be the same. You will actually get the money three, sometimes four months after the date up to which sales, including sub-licences and subsidiary rights, have been calculated. Authors frequently complain about this lapse of time, but, unless the payment comes later than the promised date – which, alas, it all too often does – you have to remember that on, say, 30 June, the publisher draws a line under the earnings of all the books on his list, including sub-leases and overseas sales, and only then begins to work out the percentages due to each individual author. Statements then have to be prepared for each one in time for the payment date. In a large house this is no small task. The majority of publishers (the best) account and pay every six months. An appreciable minority (the worst) account annually. In between come those who account half-yearly for the first year or two and then, when sales have probably dwindled, drop to annual accounting.

The Royalty Clause sets out the percentage you will receive on copies sold by the publisher. On home sales within the UK (and usually Eire) this will be calculated on the selling or retail price of the book. Here again the actual figures are going to vary, but if it's your first agreement for an adult book, you can expect them to start at 10 per cent, rising to 12½ per cent after the sale of anything from 2,000 to 5,000 copies and 15 per cent thereafter; sometimes 17½ per cent after another specified number, though this is now usual only for bestselling writers. There will often be a clause covering electronic rights – CD-ROMs and work published on the Internet, which should allow the author a minimum of 50 per cent, preferably more.

For children's books, the percentage will be scaled down, starting at 7½ per cent, though there's generally no good reason why it shouldn't rise to 10 per cent if sales turn out better than expected. For paperback, 7½ per cent is usual (in the UK; in the USA it can be lower), but, again, it ought to rise to 10 per cent after a – much increased – sale (in the USA it could be higher). But these are guidelines; no more. The answer could be better, or worse. If your book is going to be dreadfully expensive to produce – colour photographs? – you may have to accept lower royalties until the publisher's initial investment in production costs have been recovered.

For export – copies the publisher sells overseas – the royalty is usually reduced, on the grounds that other expenses are involved and the bookseller has to be given a bigger discount. This is frequently adjusted by the publisher's stipulating a royalty of, say, 10 per cent again but with the addition of four little words: of the price received. Let me explain.

The publisher, as we know, doesn't actually receive the selling price paid for his books in the bookshops. Booksellers buy them from him at something between 35 and 45 per cent of the retail price in the home market; increasingly, and in particular with

wholesalers, it could be more. Having learnt that, we can now forget it, because on home sales your royalties are calculated, as
we've noted, on the retail price. But on overseas sales the discount
to the bookseller can go as high as 50 per cent, usually even higher
outside Europe, nearer 60–70 per cent. So the price received
mentioned in the export bit of this clause may be half the selling
price or worse. Which means your royalties are at best halved too:
10 per cent (of the selling price) becomes 5 per cent. Simply
expressed as 10 per cent of the price received. Same thing. An
agent can often get round this, too, by negotiating all royalties on
the selling price, still reduced for overseas, but at the very least
you will know what you are getting, which you won't otherwise, as
you've no way of knowing what the actual price received was in
most cases.

Then there will be a clause covering sub-licences. You have
granted the publisher a licence to publish your book; this will give
him in turn the right to sub-lease certain rights to others: paperback, for example, or book club rights. Whether he controls subsidiary rights, like US, translation or film rights, will generally
depend on whether or not you are represented by a literary agent.
In any case, this clause will indicate the percentage of the income
which is due to you, which can vary from 90 to 50 per cent, the
publisher's highest cut – or 'commission' – being on book club and
paperback and the lowest on serial rights, your share being credited to your 'account', though in certain cases it may be possible to
arrange to collect it as it is earned without waiting for the next
accounting period. If you have a strong case, argue it, provided
your account is 'in credit', meaning that the advance has been
earned.

The Termination Clause should provide for the cancellation of
the agreement if the publisher goes bust or, which is somewhat
more likely, your book goes out of print, in which case provision is
made for the rights to revert to you after a certain period, which

allows the publisher time to reprint if he so wishes. This is linked to the Remainder Clause, which permits the publisher to sell surplus copies of your book at a knock-down price to a dealer when, as most contracts put it 'the demand has evidently ceased'; in other words, when nobody wants it any more. There should be a stipulation that your book won't be remaindered too soon after publication, say, for a couple of years. Most publishers allow the author 10 per cent of the remainder price if copies are sold above cost, but as they almost never are this is somewhat academic. A few publishers pay 10 per cent of the remainder price whatever it is, but at the time of writing this not many do. One important rider, not always included, is that the author should himself be offered copies at the remainder price before they are disposed of. If you think you can flog them to your friends, it's well worth buying some. Incidentally, the remainder dealer who buys them is at liberty thereafter to sell them at whatever price he can get, paying the author nothing. I have known dealers actually sell remaindered copies at the full, original price – which makes you wonder what was wrong with the publisher who got shot of them – but very rarely.

The Option Clause tends to be fairly meaningless, usually amounting to no more than an expression of continuing interest on the part of the publisher, in which case it should not be resisted. Such a clause gives the publisher first refusal of your next work, or work of a similar nature, on terms to be mutually agreed, provided he comes up with an offer within a given time (say, six weeks). You are perfectly free to refuse his offer when it comes but, though it has never to my knowledge been tested in a court of law, there is an understanding in the trade that the author is not free to accept a matching or lower offer from another publisher, only a higher one. This again seems fair to me. Two things to look out for here: occasionally the clause doesn't leave the terms to be mutually agreed but states they will be the same as for the present contract (your next book may be a blockbuster, and you are advised not to accept this); and, secondly, some options are for two books, not just one (this is OK, provided it is stipulated that if the first option isn't taken up the second option automatically lapses, otherwise you could have an unsaleable MS on your hands, because another publisher, who might like the rejected book, probably won't take it if he knows it's a once-off since the next book has to go back to the first publisher).

The Libel Warranty Clause is important too and deserves a section all to itself (see Libel on page 163).

Copyright

In the UK copyright in the written word doesn't have to be conferred by any legal process, registration or even publication; it exists automatically. If you write a letter to me, as soon as I receive it that letter belongs to me. You cannot demand it back. If you are famous and the letter – signed or, better still, handwritten by you – becomes valuable, I can, if I wish, sell it. What neither I nor anyone else can do without your permission is publish it or, for that matter, copy or translate it. The physical letter is mine; the copyright remains yours.

Copyright, though intangible, is really a property. You can assign it to someone else – give it away or sell it. But no one has the right to take it from you or use it for his own purposes, so long as the copyright lasts, which is normally up to seventy-five years after the author's death or, if the work is published posthumously, after the date of first publication.

You may assign copyright with strings attached, retaining an interest in whatever financial rewards it produces thereafter, which is what happens when you sell the copyright to a publisher (other than for an outright, once-off fee). But once you've parted with the copyright you no longer control any rights; you can't yourself sell any part of it to anyone else unless and until the new owner reassigns it back to you. For this reason most agents advise strongly against parting with the copyright in your work, unless it is some relatively minor effort, like an essay written especially for a symposium – but think of your collected works!

Your MS, incidentally, unlike the letter you sent with it, doesn't belong to the publisher and he will, if you wish, return it to you when the printer has finished with it. It's worth a thought, because authors' MSS can become valuable.

International copyright can lead us into very murky waters indeed, when for instance the nationality of the author, the country in which the book is written and the country in which the book is first published don't coincide; but for the average author copyright is protected in the most important markets throughout the world by printing in the book on first publication the symbol © followed by the name of the copyright holder and the year of first publication. Unless you have assigned the copyright, make sure that your name appears correctly in this formula in the corrected proofs before the book finally goes to press. Before the Universal Copyright Convention which laid this down, and previous conventions, books could be 'pirated' abroad quite legally and were. Unfortunately this still occurs and, though strenuous efforts are being made to enforce the law, it is extremely difficult to police in some cases, depending on the attitude of the government of the country concerned.

Libel

Your publishing agreement will have a warranty clause, which may say you guarantee the work to be your own original work, that you haven't published it elsewhere and are entitled to grant the various rights and so on. What it will certainly say is that, if it turns out to be libellous, you will be responsible for all and any damages and costs that may result – the publisher's as well as your own. For some reason obscenity gets lumped in with libel in the clause, which seems unfair, since the publisher ought to be able to spot obscenity as well as you can, which isn't necessarily true of libel. There are all sorts of alarming implications, depending on the wording of the clause, and a good agent may be able to whittle them down and protect you to some extent, but he won't be able to absolve you from responsibility for a genuine libel, and no publisher I know of will sign an agreement without this basic warranty.

As usual, running with the hare and hunting with the hounds, I have to say there's ample justification for this rigid attitude. The aggrieved party who is suing will sue author and publisher both, jointly and severally (and often the printer too!), and, as publishers tend to be richer than authors, guess who is going to have to pay up if you lose the case or settle. True, most publishers will be insured against such an eventuality; indeed, a number of publishers now insure their authors against libel and copyright claims, but there will always be those who look to the author to indemnify them. The author, incidentally, may be required to go along with any way in which the insurer proposes to deal with a claim, and the insurance may well be contingent on this. In real life, in the event of a successful claim where the author is liable to foot the bill, it generally ends up with a negotiated settlement; but it could still cost you a frightening amount.

If anything you write in your book involves a libel risk, but can't be expurgated without real loss to your argument, then either you or your publisher (for you will be well advised to alert him, if he doesn't know already) should take legal advice – and follow it. The publisher may decide to take advice anyway, and will be within his rights in refusing to publish if the advice is against it.

That's if you know there's a risk. Unfortunately you may not, because there is such a thing as accidental libel and, though this will mitigate the damages, it won't necessarily absolve you from responsibility altogether. If, in all innocence, you invent a character called Herman Hazelnut and mention that he is a well-known bigamist who lives in Upper Twistleton, and up trots a real Mr Hazelnut of Upper Twistleton who has never committed bigamy in his life, you could end up in court. The same would apply if his name isn't Hazelnut at all, but he does live in Twistleton and has red hair and a limp just like your character and is therefore easily identified by his neighbours. The more unlikely the name you choose, the worse it is if it turns out to be genuine. Real-life people can also be identified too by their designations, even if the names and descriptions don't fit. Unless you are writing science fiction set well in the future, don't denigrate the chief constable of a (real) county or the chairman of a (real or recognizable) firm, because in each case there is only one and he won't appreciate suggestions that he's had his fingers in the till or an affair with a neighbour's wife.

There is no satisfactory solution to this problem, only a few suggestions. If, as often happens, you are basing fictitious characters on real, living persons, then change them in such a way that they couldn't reasonably be identifiable. Change the colour of their hair, their age or nationality – even their sex. If your character is taken from one of the professions, like the Army, Church, medicine or Parliament, you can – and should – check in the appropriate lists which are available to make sure no such person really exists.

You can't libel a dead person, but you can be sued if your defamation implicates others, who can claim injury as a result. If you say X never did marry his supposed wife, have a thought for their offspring.

If you are dealing with real life, as opposed to fiction, you are of course free to express an opinion, however insulting, provided it is clearly an opinion and not presented as a fact, which could be disproved. Whether a man is a swindler depends on whether or not he has ever swindled anybody. Whether or not he is an ass is an opinion and not subject to proof, but you need to be careful. If calling him an ass implies, say, professional incompetence, he could still sue you.

A truism to end up with, very familiar to lawyers: the greater the truth, the greater the libel. There are basically three defences against a libel suit: one is that what you have written is fair comment on a matter of public interest – usually applied to journalism – being an honest opinion based on facts accurately stated or referred to in the text and not actuated by an improper motive; the second is to prove that what you have said is true – as in the famous Oscar Wilde case – but the onus is on you to prove it; the third is to show that the inference drawn by the aggrieved party is unreasonable – you didn't mean it or him and no reasonable person would infer that you did.

Lawyers

If you need to go to a solicitor, find one who specializes in the book trade. Very few do. If you need to seek counsel's opinion, he will know the right barrister for you, a specialist again, as counsel invariably is. Despite the popular interest in book publishing, as evinced in the press, in terms of the wide world of business it's pretty small fry, and I dare say there isn't room for too many specialists. Divorce would be a better bet for the articled clerk.

Publishing agreements, though they look complex when you first run into them, are mostly, in legalistic terms, fairly loose and imprecise: almost gentlemen's agreements. A razor-keen, non-specialist lawyer can ride horses and carts through them, and will, ending up with something twenty times as long-winded and providing for every eventuality, however remote. The specialist will save you that, well aware of the customs of the trade, which will be recognized in law. I once had an author who assigned her copyright, and therefore all earnings, to a charity. The charity's own lawyers drew up a deed of assignment, based on the original publishing agreement. It ran to some twelve pages. With their approval I reduced it to three. Any experienced agent or publisher will know a great deal more about his business than the average lawyer – nothing clever in this; it's true of all professionals who are expert in their trade, as they must be – but a whole lot less than the specialist lawyer, especially when it comes to abstruse subjects like international copyright and libel. I'm not suggesting that the average lawyer will give you bad advice (or that he won't) but that you will save yourself time and money by finding the right one.

12 Rights

In our brief look at agreements we considered your book as a house, which you leased out, either wholly or piecemeal, and what you leased were the rights. Let's take a closer look at some of the more important ones.

US rights

If your book is under contract to a British publisher and is of possible interest to the US market – which something on cricket or walks in Wessex won't be – either your publisher or your agent, or just possibly you yourself, will want to approach US publishers. If your publisher controls US rights he may deal direct – if your book is one of a series already committed to a US publisher he almost certainly will. However, the approach is nearly always made through a US literary agent, no matter who controls the rights – unless the UK publisher has a branch in the USA.

It is usual for the US publisher to offset the British edition – reproducing by photography from a British copy, with his own imprint – which doesn't affect the author except when, as sometimes happens, some British-English words and phrases might change meaning or become less than comprehensible when they cross the Atlantic, in which case the text may be modified to a 'mid-Atlantic' compromise before it goes to the printer in the first place. An offset fee is paid – not to the author – which is considerably less than the cost of setting up and producing the book all over again, so everyone is happy. Occasionally, if the Americans don't like the British edition, or can't agree on modifications in the text, they may produce an independent edition, but this is a less attractive proposition, and the need for it could reduce the chances of a sale. The same process applies when a British publisher buys an American book.

The best American contract is a parallel to the English one. The Americans buy US rights and pay an advance and royalties in the normal way. There will be a new agreement, either between the publishers or, if you have an agent or are dealing direct, between the US publisher and you. Canada can go either way, usually with the first to publish, as it is both Commonwealth and territorially American.

Second best is a deal whereby the Americans import finished copies – bound up, with their imprint on the title page in place of the British one – or sheets – unbound pages, to be bound up there – both of which indicate that they anticipate only modest sales which wouldn't justify republishing themselves even by offset. (If they sell out, they can always order more.) Such deals are almost always on a 'royalty inclusive' basis, meaning that the American buyer isn't going to pay the author anything: the author's percentage has to come from the British publisher's profit on the sale. Since bound copies and sheets are sold at a figure not greatly above cost, as a rule, and the author's royalty will be based on the 'price received', it means a poor return. All one can say is that it's better than nothing. It does reduce the British publisher's investment – sometimes quite considerably – not so much from his profit margin on the actual sale but on his extended print run: the longer the print run the cheaper the 'unit cost', the printer's charge per copy.

Publishers are, therefore, much happier to accept second best than the author or agent is.

Serial rights

You will know that extracts from books are sometimes published in a newspaper, magazine or journal. Immediately before the book comes out is the ideal time: for some curious reason this tends to stimulate sales rather than kill them, either because the 'serial' – the publication of extracts – contains only part of it and the reader is inspired to want to read the whole, or because he never got round to reading the serial but remembers having noticed it, and seeing the book rings a bell. Serial publication too soon before the book appears is a lot less useful, because serial readers have short memories; after book publication doesn't work too well either, because editors of periodicals don't like their material second-hand – and pay much less for it. Serial rights for your book will be controlled by you (your agent) or by the publisher on a relatively modest commission; either way, there's no problem provided the extracts aren't too extensive. It is possible to publish a condensed form of the book in one issue. This is known as a 'one-shot', and the publisher's approval will be necessary and his cut will be greater – up to 50 per cent – because this could arguably cut into book sales. Serial publication of the whole book in its entirety will land you in trouble, if not in court, for reasons perfectly obvious but legally horribly complicated – hinging on what constitutes 'volume rights' – which we won't go into.

I said 'in one issue' just now. One thinks of 'serial' as referring to something published at intervals, in a series, and so it does. But it actually refers to the periodical not to the content. If you sell a short story to a magazine, you are still selling serial rights.

Serial rights are customarily sold and acquired by an exchange of letters, without a formal contract, but you should make sure that you retain copyright and that you have specified exactly what 'serial rights' you are parting with, because there is more than one kind. In Britain, the most common are First British Serial Rights (FBSR), which for your part guarantees that you won't allow anyone else to publish in this form before it – the acquiring periodical – does (First) in Britain (British), and for the periodical's part allows them to publish the material once and once only, after which they have no further interest. Occasionally the buyer, especially a newspaper, and particularly in the case of an original short story, will ask if they may have in addition 'syndication rights'. If you agree, this will allow them to resell your story (or whatever) to other newspapers (or wherever) on a commission basis (usually 50 per cent, but it may be negotiated). Unless you have a better idea, I'd be very much in favour of agreeing to this: the result won't make your fortune, but it will in many cases bring in a modest return which you otherwise wouldn't get. A short story I sold once to a London newspaper with syndication rights was subsequently resold to papers in Eire and Ceylon (as it was then) and other places I now disremember, but certainly in places I could never have offered it myself. But it was hardly a major literary effort and, if yours is, retain these rights by all means.

In practice, the rights a periodical normally insists on are those that cover the area in which their periodical is actually sold. Certain magazines, and particularly American ones, require first world serial rights. You can see why. If it's an American magazine that publishes an edition in Britain, the last thing they want is to publish a story or piece which has already appeared in a British magazine.

Some literary agents will charge you more than the basic 10 per cent for handling serial rights in a short story. I expect you can see why this is, too.

Translation rights

If your book is of potential interest to readers in a foreign country (and language), your agent or your publisher will want to offer it to publishers there, usually through the good offices of a literary agent working in the country concerned. Many foreign publishers regularly see British publishers' lists or British trade publications and will ask to be sent copies of books they think might suit their own. They will read them or have them read (in English of course) and, if they buy the rights, will be responsible for having them translated.

The author's new agreement should stipulate that the translation must be faithful and so on, but the choice of the translator remains firmly with the publishers, who will choose someone he knows from experience will do a good job. Only very rarely will he be open to suggestions on this.

Book club rights

Book clubs, as we all know, supply their members with books, often identical to the original edition, at a much reduced price, often a fraction of what one would have to pay in a bookshop. How do they do this?

Booksellers used to be bound by agreement with the publishers, called the Net Book Agreement, not to sell their books at less than the price fixed by the publisher. Now the NBA has been abandoned, supermarkets, like book clubs, can fix their own price. To make a profit, this obviously means they buy them from the publishers at a high discount, for which there will be reduced royalties. Authors and agents tend to grumble a great deal about this, and some authors indeed have simply refused to accept a book club deal. If your agreement requires your approval (as it should), and you feel strongly about it (as you well may), you can always refuse too.

But don't be too hasty.

In the first place it can be argued, with a lot of truth, that the members who subscribe to the book club buy books they would otherwise never dream of buying at the full price. Where this is true, the publisher and author are not losing regular sales. So it's a bonus, however modest. Secondly, book club members receive publicity material regularly, drawing their attention to books they might otherwise never have been aware of; and they joined the club in the first place because it supplies the sort of books they are interested in. There's no guarantee that they would otherwise browse through bookshops in search of them or would find them even if they did.

Thirdly, though the publisher's actual remuneration from the club may be modest, a decent book club order will enable him to increase his own print run, thereby reducing his unit cost. It may enable him to bring the retail price of his own edition down, which, though you may not believe it, is almost invariably in the author's interest because of the likelihood of greatly increased sales. In some extreme cases, the publisher may actually rely on an order from a club to make his publication viable: no book club, no deal.

Finally, the worst that can happen is that it increases the author's readership and promotes his name, which is worth bearing in mind.

There are over fifty book clubs in Great Britain, most of the major ones controlled by such groups as Book Club Associates and the Readers' Union, catering for most tastes, and others supplying through schools especially for children. There are two main kinds: those that publish simultaneously with the publisher's own edition – but of course selling only to members – and those that issue reprints of books after they have had a regular sale.

In addition, there are specialist companies which, under licence from the publishers, produce their own editions in large print for readers with poor eyesight. These, happily, really don't affect normal sales and are especially popular with libraries (see Public Lending Right on page 196).

The book clubs usually pay a royalty of 10 per cent of their selling price, which isn't a lot, but the useful aspect is that they generally pay an advance equal to this royalty on their entire first edition 'up front'.

If, as with the large-print companies, the books themselves are not supplied by the publishers, then clearly the publisher won't benefit from reducing his unit cost; but, against that, he has as it were nothing to lose and a little something to gain, as has the author, who in this case should receive a minimum of 50 per cent of the licence fee.

13 Editorial

There are many facets of your publishing house with which you as author will have little or no direct contact, at least initially: production, design, finance and accounts, rights, publicity, public relations, sales and marketing, for example. Publicity certainly can – and should – come into your orbit later on, and so may some others, but initially your contact is with Editorial: the all-important editor.

Or editors, I should say. The term is somewhat imprecise and varies from publisher to publisher. The editor who actually takes your book on, sometimes called the acquisitions editor if he or she is called anything special, may or may not be the one to go over the text with you before it goes off to the printer; you may be assigned another editor within the firm or a freelance. This is the important one, in practical terms, especially for the new author. (There may also be a desk editor lurking in the background, whom you won't meet, whose job it is to prepare your typescript for the printer with all sorts of technical instructions regarding the actual typeface, layout, etc.)

One way or another, though, you will meet up with 'your' editor, and I hope you will be friends.

Plainly the publishers like your book, or they wouldn't have accepted it. Sometimes revision is a condition of acceptance – a common condition might be to reduce the length – but even if it isn't there is a strong probability that your editor, having gone through the MS line by line, will come up with suggestions for improvement, and you would be very foolish indeed not to give them very careful consideration.

Most MSS, even by experienced authors, can be improved by skilful editing – by the author on reflection; it can be done by the editor alone, but this is unusual and undesirable generally (unless you are about to disappear to Outer Mongolia or you get run over by a bus, in which case your estate will probably have to pay for the editor's time). If the editor does make amendments to your text, you should insist on approving the alterations. More usually the editor will make suggestions for the author to consider. Bear in mind that your editor has read hundreds and hundreds of books and has a professional eye for weak points and that you, the author, will be much too close to your book to see it objectively.

Don't be unreasonable and insist on your original version unless you genuinely feel strongly that you are right. On the other hand, don't be bullied into accepting changes you hate. One author I looked after had her book lined up for publication both in Britain and the USA; both editors had copies of the MS and both bombarded her with proposed amendments, by no means always the same ones. She wrote cynically that if they got together they would no doubt write a smashing book between them; but meanwhile this one was hers.

Quite right too. But you may like to know that not a few of our bestselling authors owe a great deal to their editors and rely on them to help give their books that final, professional polish at the very least.

One last point. It is unreasonable to expect or to rely on your editor to pick up misspellings, grammatical errors or misquotations, let alone errors of fact in non-fiction which you could have picked up yourself. Leave him or her to deal with those you missed unintentionally.

House style

Do you write summer or south with a capital S?

Do you write five hundred pounds or £500? Five hundred dollars or $500?

Do you use single or double quotation marks for dialogue?

Do you care?

If you don't – and there's usually no good reason why you should, since none is incorrect – use whichever comes to mind and leave it to your publishers to change it if they want to. They might.

For the sake of convenience – and consistency – most if not all publishers decide early on which alternatives they happen to prefer and draw up a list – some will even send you a copy. This constitutes their 'house style'. The desk editor who prepared your MS for the printer will follow it, altering your text where it doesn't conform. Normally.

The majority of authors are content to accept their publisher's house style. However, if you have taken considerable trouble over the minutiae and consider them important, you don't have to. In which case you should mark your MS 'Follow Copy'.

It could land you in the soup.

If you stipulate 'Follow Copy' the editor and printer may well do just that. Warts and all. I stipulated it once for sound reasons: I omitted dialogue quotes altogether in the French style because I wanted deliberately to blur the distinction between what characters were saying and thinking; but that was a rare case. When the proofs arrived for the usual author's approval, I found – to give a small example of the hazards you could be in for – a word I had misspelled left as it was, with a question mark in the margin as if to say, 'Do you really want it spelled like this?' (No, I didn't.) This sort of thing can be expensive (see Proofs on page 180). Of course, if your own ideas are too eccentric, your publisher may object and you'll have to argue it out.

All this applies, of course, to the general run of books, where the text is the important thing, which won't in any case be much affected by the minutiae or the layout. If illustrations, graphics or design are a vital constituent, then contrariwise you may well want to be involved from the start, and should be, and will put forward your ideas for discussion at least.

Proofs

You and your editor between you should get your MS into near-perfect shape in house before the edited book goes to the printer; but mistakes do slip through the net. The printer will produce a specimen for approval before going full steam ahead. For a book, this will mean a small number of copies known as 'uncorrected proofs', which look like rather crude paperbacks and are also called 'page proofs'. If your book is complicated, especially in design, the proofs may appear in 'galley' form, looking like an unwound, outsize loo roll, not yet divided into pages, or in bound galleys, like an outsize book in length; or in other photographic forms. You should get two; one to amend if necessary and one to keep for reference.

Most major numbers of publishers now undertake pre-press production 'in house' including computer design and typesetting. This may mean that there is more latitude for making changes to the text at proof stage without incurring major costs, though authors should check with their editors before radically altering proofs.

Your publisher will send you a proof of your book as soon as it comes off the press for your corrections and amendments. Your agreements may require you to correct proofs and return them within, say, a couple of weeks. It is your right in any case to examine them, though you may waive this if, for example, you're going to be abroad or desperately busy – in which case you can't blame anybody else if errors occur in the printed book. But normally your job is to read through the proof carefully, comparing it where necessary with the second copy of your MS you should have kept by you, and to do two or three things.

First, correct any mistakes that may have introduced *after* you last saw the text. This is where your copy of the MS comes in. Was it your mistake or someone else's? If not yours, you won't be charged for the correction.

Secondly, correct any mistakes that originated in your MS, the ones that slipped through the net. At this stage you may also change your mind and alter things you wrote originally to something you like better. In either case, you will be charged for the resetting. If outside typesetters are being used rather than the book being set in house by the publisher, then 10 per cent, sometimes 15 per cent of the original setting costs will be allowed free; this sounds a lot but isn't, as alterations can be enormously expensive – though now that text is laid out digitally rather than more traditional methods, such as 'hot metal', it is a much easier job. If you must rewrite at proof stage, the best way to keep the cost down is to substitute new text of the same length as the text removed. The substitution can then be made without disturbing the page setting as a whole. If your revision markedly alters the length of the line in which it appears, it could mean readjusting the following line, several lines, a whole paragraph or even a page. Again, this is less of a problem than it used to be, though, if there's an index and it's already been done by this stage, then it could throw out the numbering and you could be writing a blank cheque for excess corrections.

We've been considering uncorrected proofs, and the proofs at this stage will be just that: the proofs from the same initial print run, which your publisher may be offering for the sale of rights (paperback, US, book clubs and so on, pre-publication) or sent out for publicity purposes. The first proof you receive, however, may have some corrections already marked by the publisher's own reader. If the rules are followed, these may be marked in red ink (probably ballpoint), or green for typesetters' marks and queries. The corrections thus far will be compositors' errors, such as require an eagle's eye to spot sometimes, like wrong fonts. You should mark your corrections or amendments in blue to distinguish one from the other. If you find typesetters' errors which have been overlooked, then use a different colour again. The important thing is to distinguish the corrections which are your fault, for which you will be charged, from those which aren't, for which you won't.

Indexes

– or indices, if you prefer, it's optional. If your book requires one, your agreement will in all probability require you either to prepare it yourself or, failing that, to bear the cost of having a professional indexer do it for you. Whether an index is required or not should be decided by your publisher and you. As professional indexers are well paid, do it yourself if you can – you will then understand why they are well paid. This will also have the advantage that the result will be what you wanted.

If you haven't tackled an index before, have a look at some of the many published books that have them. If it's a book you've read, and you now realize that the index was helpful and well organized, so much the better. But any fairly comprehensive index should give you the idea. What it won't do is to tell you how it was achieved.

One method is to buy a simple card-index system: a set of ruled cards with alphabetical divisions, preferably boxed so they don't slide about and end up on the floor. When you get your uncorrected – or in your case partially corrected – page proof, in the course of reading it through, keep the second copy by your side in parallel – this is the one not corrected at all – and underline or highlight any name, place or any other item appropriate for the index, at the same time jotting it down under its initial letter with the page number on the appropriate card. Use a separate card for each entry. As you read on, each time that item crops up all you have to do is to add the page number on its card. When you reach the end of the proof, bingo, you have an index.

The trick here is to know what to put in and what to leave out. Keep in mind the main theme of your book and the salient points; also the names of people and places that play a not unimportant part, selecting those entries most likely to be of interest to your reader. Or potential reader: he may well consult the index before buying the book, and if your book is a biography of Napoleon and there's nothing under Waterloo, or a book on heresies and no listing of Albigensian, it may be regarded as a non-starter, even if these important items *are* to be found in the text.

If, as may happen, you need the index before the book is in page proof, then you will need to underline the relevant items on the typescript itself, in which case the page numbers won't of course coincide with those in the printed book. But it might in any case be a useful exercise to sort out what to include.

Jackets

– usually called dust covers – and paperback covers, which are an integral part of the book. Your publisher may show you a design or proof of yours before it's printed. He may invite your approval and even, if you're lucky, listen to you when you tell him you hate it. (I remember one author's reaction to the finished copy, which was to congratulate the publisher on a superb piece of camouflage: he said he'd put the book in his bookshelf and afterwards couldn't find it.) What the publisher won't do is to let you have the last word.

I have to admit, there are good reasons for this. In the first place, the author isn't always the best judge. An aesthetically pleasing jacket illustration or design might not stand out at all in a bookshop, buried among hundreds of competing titles. And secondly, if the final word were with the author, he or she could go on rejecting designs endlessly, which would not only be expensive, it could also hold up production and publication.

Complain, if you get the chance, if the jacket is illustrated and the illustration is actually wrong: the heroine is a brunette, not a blonde; the aircraft has the wrong markings. You ought to be consulted in any case, but if you have suggestions make them early.

Naturally, if the final jacket was your choice, if you won the argument and the book thereafter fails to sell, you will be open to the inevitable 'I told you so.'

Blurbs

The rather vulgar-sounding word for the bits on the inside flaps of dust jackets, on the backs of paperbacks and probably also in the publisher's catalogue announcing forthcoming titles, which tells you what the book is all about.

I was once sent the draft blurb for one of my own books for approval. Publishers don't always or even commonly do this, but ask to see it if you get the chance. Mine was so awful that I rewrote it myself and, though it didn't finally appear in quite the glowing terms of my version, it did convey the sense I'd intended. Nobody knows your book as well as you do, and if you suggest to your publisher that you would like to draft your own blurb you may be surprised to find he not only agrees but is delighted. It's much easier to work on another's draft than to concoct something from scratch. In fact, it would be a good idea if publishers, once they have accepted a MS and sent the author a questionnaire – as most do and all should – asking for background details that could be useful in promoting the book, at the same time invited the author to submit a draft blurb.

Design

The design or layout of your book will normally be left to the publisher's discretion. He will decide what typeface to choose – often in practice dependent on what is readily available; the more exotic ones may not be – the width of margin spaces and in general whether the production is going to be mean or lavish. If he is a sensible publisher, his decision will be the right one, linked as always to the potential sale, print run and retail price. If you have strong feelings about this, make them clear before you sign an agreement; don't wait to complain when you see the book in print.

In most cases this won't materially affect your book anyway: the text is the thing. But if your book involves illustrations or design which form an integral part of it you may well be directly involved.

For children's books, as we've noted, you may not be. They are, at least for older children, an embellishment and could probably be omitted altogether without too serious a loss. But for adult books they could be essential, in which case you should certainly be consulted and will probably be called upon to work with the publisher's design department.

In the case of photographs, they may be inserted throughout the book – situated where they relate to the text – or they may be lumped together in groups or sections. Authors prefer the first; the second is less expensive to produce. In the end it comes down, once again, to what production costs the book will stand in relation to the retail price.

14 Sales

How is your book actually sold? Well, of course, customers go into bookshops and buy it; either because they see it on display and like the look of it or because they know about it already and specifically ask for it. The first obviously depends on your book's being in the shop in the first place. But so, to a great extent, does the second. The customer may be prepared to wait while the bookseller orders a copy from the publisher, but there is a chance that he won't. So it's in everybody's interests to have the book in the shop on publication day. How does your publisher set about this?

Mainly, in three ways.

First, he produces a seasonal catalogue, or 'list' of forthcoming books from his house, well ahead of publication – usually quarterly – which goes out to all the main booksellers, giving them ample time to order copies. (You should get a copy of the list too.)

Secondly, he will, with few exceptions, list forthcoming titles in the trade journal, the *Bookseller*, which again virtually all booksellers have to have. He may even place a special advertisement for your book. In any case, he will list it among his forthcoming publications in one of the bulk seasonal issues. A good bookseller will go through these and note the titles he plans to order.

Thirdly your publisher's reps will call on the main booksellers with their list, to take orders and try to persuade the booksellers to order your book.

In addition, as we have seen, your book may be promoted through websites and online catalogues.

From this basic approach, you can see that booksellers generally have no excuse for claiming ignorance of your book, even if they have to look it up, and have every opportunity to order copies.

Which is a far cry from saying that it will be in the shop. The horse has well and truly been led to the water. But will he drink?

Only a very few of the very largest bookshops can possibly stock more than a tiny percentage of the books offered to them, as we know, and, of these, books by well-established authors whose books have a more or less guaranteed sale will take priority and thus reduce the percentage still more. The bookseller must, therefore, have a good reason for ordering copies of your book, out of an enormous number of others queuing up for attention, and this is where publicity and promotion comes into it. Big publishers can exert pressure on shops to take more obscure titles by getting them in on the back of sure-fire sellers, as well as by buying window and table space and giving huge discounts for bulk orders.

Put yourself in the publisher's place, and, for that matter, in the bookseller's place, too. If you have any bright ideas for lifting your book out of the common and over-populated rut, don't be shy of putting them forward. Only, if they involve expense, remember that this will have to go into the costing of the book and have to make financial sense and not simply increase the publisher's risk.

Most general books are supplied to booksellers on 'sale or return'; that is, unsold copies may be returned to the publisher and credited, when the author's royalty will be debited, and your agreement will have a clause providing for this. The right to return should be for a limited period only, though some shops now have returns targets which, if they are not met, can affect their monthly budgets for buying new books, and this difficulty can in turn be put at the publisher's door by the shop's refusing to take any more books until requests to return – reasonable or unreasonable – are authorized.

Advertising and promotion

Publishers will sometimes tell you they advertise their books only in order to please the authors. This sounds like a singularly feeble excuse for doing next to nothing, and you may be surprised to learn that it's quite often true; or at least better than a half-truth.

An advertisement for your book in the popular press will be competing with others, and these are usually limited to 'lead titles', that is,. those expecting substantial sales anyway. Each title will rate perhaps a couple of lines telling the interested reader why he should rush out and buy it. Of course, almost nobody does any such thing. Advertisements in the trade press will list forthcoming titles, not yet published, and sometimes promote single books in the hope that booksellers will order copies, but the circulation is much, much smaller than the national press and the competition intense.

I don't myself accept this as a valid reason for not advertising at all (*pace* a distinguished female publisher who assured me that her policy was to spend the money on employing reps of the highest quality, who were magnificent at getting the books into the bookshops, which is what really counts. I saw this as 'blinding you with science' – she was good at that – since the agent has no way of verifying this plausible statement). I still think that a publisher should advertise every book, however modestly, if only because there's a chance that someone out there really needs to know, not how marvellous it is but that it's been published and if it isn't in the local bookshop that it can at least be ordered. This especially applies of course when it's not the author's first book, and he or she really may have fans who want to know when the next book is available.

Authors are frequently frustrated at the apparent lack of real effort on the part of their publishers. 'If only they'd promoted my book properly, it would have sold like hot cakes.' Possibly; one can't prove a negative. But probably not. Supposing they had gone all out to promote it. Supposing it had then created a tremendous demand. That would be splendid, provided they had printed sufficient copies to meet the demand. If they hadn't, and it's gone out of print, potential customers will be told they can order a copy of the reprint which will be available in six weeks or six months. Do you imagine they will wait, rather than buy something else? If you are following me, you will appreciate that expensive and extensive advertising is practical only when the publishers have substantial stocks of your book, taking up costly warehouse space, not to mention the initial investment, in anticipation of booming sales. If the demand never comes, they are well and truly lumbered. Unwanted books are either sold off to remainder dealers, as we've seen, in which case the publisher is unusually lucky of he recovers the bare cost of printing them, or pulped, when he certainly won't. For some reason books aren't like normal shop goods, and knocking 10 or 15 per cent off the original price won't shift them, unless they are bestsellers already.

If you remember, I mentioned in a previous section a barrister client of mine who quarrelled with the form of publishing agreements. I've also represented authors who worked in advertising. Without exception they were scornfully convinced that publishers had no idea. We can all agree that a skilfully concocted advertisement for a first-class product points towards lots more sales than a poor one for an indifferent product. But, as I'm sure any advertising executive will tell you, virtually any professional advert will result in increased sales, and I believe this to be absolutely true. True, too, that if the increased sales don't cover the cost of the advertising, something has gone wrong somewhere. And the sad fact is that the profit margin on the average book leaves little scope, if any, for an advertising budget. The profit margin is what the publisher has left from the money he receives from booksellers and others, after allowing for the author's royalty, the printing and overheads like a share of his rent, rates, salaries, etc.

But my authors-in-advertising never had to promote a one-off and inexpensive product like a single book. Imagine launching an entirely new detergent at regular intervals to a public who would only buy it once! It is possible to advertise a publisher's whole list as such, and Mills and Boon have done it very successfully on the basis that if you like one you will probably like all the others; but this doesn't apply to most publishers.

I'm not of course talking about proven or even potential best-sellers, which may rate a quite extensive advertising budget, even a ten-second spot on television at enormous cost. And at this level advertising can indeed work, on the well-tried principle that nothing succeeds like success. Put in simple terms, an advertisement that says this is a marvellous book cuts not a lot of ice. If it puts the words in quotes, endorsed by a well-known authority or celebrity, it will be a bit more effective (see Puffs on page 192). If it is quoting from an important review, for instance from a national rather than provincial paper, better still; but we're still in a low league. If the publishers, though, can splash about the fact that a US publisher has bought rights for a million dollars, paperback rights have been sold for a similarly enormous sum, the film is being signed up and serial rights have been acquired by a top newspaper – this really does ginger up sales no end. Nobody likes to miss out on what they are persuaded everybody else is talking about – the hype – because what sells books is getting them talked about. Most often an editorial comment or feature article – which is the job of the public relations side – is much more effective than a paid advertisement. Unfortunately, what makes good 'copy' in journalism is not the quality of the book but the fact that it made the author a dollar millionaire, that he or she is newsworthy – celebrity value again – in which case the article will be about the author rather than about the book, unless the subject of the book itself is of interest to a specific readership, which usually means non-fiction: a new way to cook spaghetti or how to avoid a heart attack. But basically, something that lends itself to a news story, which fiction usually doesn't. Quality doesn't come into it. Your publisher will, or should, explore this public relations side if he is equipped to do so or may employ a professional PR person to handle it for a fee. But you can see the problem if you yourself are a rather average sort of person and all you've done is to write a fine novel. If the publisher can quote someone well known to say it's the best thing since sliced bread it helps, but as everybody does this the effect is limited.

Still, publishers will, or again should, ask you for a list of the names of people you know to whom they can send advance copies (pre-publication), who might be useful in publicizing your work, and, if you have useful connections make the most of them. They may give a puff or be influential in getting a mention in a journal or on radio or even making a display in their bookshop.

Your publisher could hold a launch party for your book. I expect this will cross your mind. The idea is, of course, to invite the press along and get lots of write-ups and publicity.

This, like signing parties in bookshops, is of dubious value in terms of value-for-money unless you are already a famous author or somebody people are dying to meet anyway. Film stars who write novels are a good bet. A signing party is embarrassing if only two women and a dog turn up.

If you are determined and rich enough, you can always subsidize the advertising, parties or whatever, yourself. I've known authors to at least share the cost of the junketings, and most publishers would go along with this, within reason. There is no harm in it. If you recover the expense in terms of increased royalties, I'd say you're lucky.

Puffs

The trade word for pre-publication comments on your book from suitable people whose name and praise will help promote the book. That's the idea, anyway. They are something the publisher can quote even before the reviews start to come in. He may print the comment – or the most flattering part of it – in his initial advertising, on the book's jacket or, if it arrives too late, on an added band wrapped around it. If it's good and long enough he may publish it in the book itself; but then it's properly not a puff but an introduction or preface.

Apart from catching the eye of the potential book-buyer, the idea is that if the puff is by someone terribly eminent who says it's marvellous, book reviewers will hesitate to say it's rotten – though in fact they often take a malicious delight in doing just that. Still, puffs can be useful in giving your book a kind of imprimatur by someone who knows what he's talking about, which is better than the obviously biased praise from the publisher's own publicity department, sometimes even quoted from the blurb which may have been written by the author himself.

Puffs are not all that easy to come by, bearing in mind that they are not paid for. Introductions and prefaces usually are paid for; not that that's the incentive, like a kind of bribe – they're not paid enough for that – but the payment covers to some extent the time and trouble. So you and your publisher are relying on good-will and genuine appreciation. True, if the eminent person is asked to report on the book, he will be paid, and if the report is a good one he may allow himself to be quoted. But he isn't being paid to be nice about it, and if he didn't like it he won't be.

If your publisher believes your book will appeal strongly to someone suitably distinguished and approachable, he may ask if he or she will agree to read it. Naturally, if the resultant comments are unfavourable, everyone quietly forgets it.

If you, the author, know of a potential puffer who is kindly disposed towards you and shares your tastes or opinions, you yourself can give the thing a leg up. Do by all means.

15 Financial

Sooner or later as a professional author you are going to need an accountant to sort out your tax returns and probably Value Added Tax, too (see Value Added Tax on page 196). If possible, choose one who already acts for authors and is familiar with the peculiarities of your business. I say one because, though the bigger firms look prestigious, they will charge more, and you are more than likely to get an articled clerk on your doorstep rather than one of the partners. On the other hand, if they already look after the affairs of some vast business whose chairman happens to be your uncle, you may be taken in on grace-and-favour terms, which is all to the good.

Any competent, professional accountant will ensure that all the various returns you make will be satisfactory to the Inland Revenue. The right accountant for you may do a lot more, and actually advise you how to save money. Like a good agent, he may well save you more than the cost of his own services, which are tax-deductible anyway.

Once accepted by the Inland Revenue as a professional author – which can of course a be part-time activity but must be continuing – you will be taxed under the advantageous Schedule D as self-employed; this will enable you to claim allowances for expenses incurred in the course of your work, including the part-use of your home and its outgoings, as we have seen, research and travel and, of course, equipment. But there are pitfalls here, and as soon as you begin to earn an accountant is strongly advised.

Value Added Tax

A curious anomaly for authors, in that the better-off don't pay it and the worse-off do. Or, to be more accurate, everybody has to pay it, but only the better-off can claim it back again. If your literary income is above a certain level (the amount increases annually but, in terms of average earnings by authors, is quite high) you must register for VAT. If it is below that level, and your local VAT office (Customs and Excise) is reasonable, as they generally are, you will be allowed to register anyway if you can show that not registering would involve you in a loss of income – which it would and often does. The question is, how great a loss?

Many authors seem to regard registering for VAT in the same light as being liable to pay income tax, which it isn't. In the simplest terms, the author is charged VAT on any services he uses in the course of his business, such as his agent or his accountant, and on a great number of purchases he makes necessary for his work, big and small. (Of course he is charged VAT on other things too, not relevant to this discussion, which everybody pays.) If he isn't VAT-registered, that's the end of it.

If he is registered, his publishers will be paying him VAT on most of the money they pay him (there are exceptions, such as money received from overseas). This VAT he has paid out is deducted from the VAT received from the publishers and is due to Customs and Excise. Normally the latter would greatly exceed the former; if it isn't he will get a refund. Which is to say, he isn't paying VAT himself at all, in so far as his authorship is concerned.

The question, as I said, is, how great a loss? If the VAT you are paying is fairly little, you may prefer not to bother with all those forms and records you need to complete.

Public Lending Right

If you have had a book published with your name on the title page, though not necessarily in the copyright line, you will normally be entitled to register under this scheme, which came into operation in February 1984, and to receive an additional 'royalty' (at the time of writing 2.07 pence) on each copy, each time it is estimated that it has been loaned out from a public library, provided the total comes to more than £1 in any one year per edition of a book, with a maximum payment of £5,000.

If you're wondering how the administrators of the scheme manage to get round all the public libraries in Britain, the answer is, they don't. Thirty libraries are taken as a sample and multiplied to produce an estimate.

You won't qualify if you don't happen to be a citizen of Britain or another of the EU countries and/or don't live here; nor if you wrote the book as co-author with more than two others. If your book has one or two co-authors or an illustrator, you should try to rope him or them in to claim jointly with you, having agreed the split of the proceeds. When the scheme was first brought in, if you failed – they may have disappeared, died or be uninterested – this rendered you ineligible, but happily this condition has been rescinded and you could now qualify for a proportion of the total anyway. Translators can also now be included for PLR – which they weren't – so can compilers and editors if they have provided a minimum 10 per cent or ten pages of the text, whichever is less.

It doesn't matter when your book was published or if it's out of print; if it is still in the libraries it can still earn royalties.

Sad to say, you have to be alive at the time your registration is made; which means that widows and widowers can't claim anything.

This is a rough guide only; of course there's more to it. If you think you may qualify, write to the PLR Office, Richard House, Sorbonne Close, Stockton-on-Tees, Cleveland TS17 6DA, and you will be sent an explanatory leaflet and an Application for Registration form. Registration is a tedious business, but the rewards may surprise you.

16 Complaints: reasonable and unreasonable

Ich grolle nicht, und wenn das Herz auch bricht.

I've seen this line from Heine rather beautifully translated as 'I do not complain, no, not if the heart itself is broken', but strictly speaking *grollen* doesn't mean to complain, it means to bear a grudge. There is a difference.

Not complaining so often doesn't mean you don't bear a grudge; it means you bear a thumping great grudge and are bottling it up. This is soul-destroying and not only to the bearer of ill-will. The agent or publisher suddenly learns that the author has been nursing a grievance for the past couple of years and only now brings it to the surface. Out come the old files, correspondence and agreements, notes of telephone calls – if he's lucky enough to find them – pored over and thumbed through in search of some mishap or misunderstanding, more often than not in itself comparatively trivial and which could have been cleared up easily and painlessly at the time. Whether the complaint was justified or not has by now become irrelevant: ill-will has raised its ugly head and things will never be quite the same again. Authors are apt to feel lonely and neglected, and nothing is calculated to make you feel lonelier and more neglected than the apparent indifference of the people you're dealing with, even if they are totally unaware of it. So complain. But try to be generous with the benefits of the doubt. You'll find it will pay dividends.

Take the unanswered letter. There has to be a reason, and as you don't know what it is you invent one. Why hasn't he/she replied? 'He can't be bothered.' (A favourite, with the unthinking implication that he's had plenty of time doing nothing in particular.) 'All he's interested in is the money-spinning authors.' (Implying something like the opposite.) Or even 'He's cross with me. What did I say?' (He should know better; after all it's his job to know artists are temperamental.)

You're assuming the worst. For your own sake, assume the best. Assume the letter has gone astray in the post or went to the wrong address, or that his reply did – unlikely, but not unknown. Supposing the recipient has been run over by a bus or rushed off to have a baby; your indignant letter accusing him or her of unbusinesslike conduct is going to look pretty silly, especially if you signed yourself Joe or Jean with 'The Old Rectory' as the only heading and nobody else in the firm can work out who the hell you are. Because in many cases there may well be a good reason for the deafening silence and, even if there isn't, a polite enquiry – 'You're usually so prompt at answering letters, I was worried in case you hadn't had mine . . .' – will serve your own interests much better than a furious complaint, guaranteed to antagonize someone you want on your side. If your complaint is justified, you should receive an apology. If it isn't, I hope you will offer one. Either way, you should end up friends, the air magically cleared.

An unanswered letter is cause for complaint. So is the late payment of moneys due to you: often publishers can be, and the worst habitually are, late, but allow a reasonable interim. Book jackets can be (see Jackets on page 200), so can poor design or sloppy editorial work carried out without your approval or any of the hundred and one things that can go wrong internally within a publisher's or even an agent's office. But, if possible, complain while there is still time for remedy.

Lack of sales of your book may or may not be cause for complaint; but complaining is usually fruitless unless you can pinpoint the cause. You may assume it's for want of effort on the publisher's part, but it may be nothing of the kind. The publisher's reps should indeed be calling on at least the main book-shops and outlets. Obviously they will be trying to sell your book, along with a lot of others – most, after all, work on commission of some sort. Equally obviously, they won't always succeed; as we've seen, the great majority of bookshops can stock only a tiny per-centage of the books published every season, or even every week. But it may be worse than that.

You – or more probably a friend – went into a bookshop and asked for your book and they had never heard of it. Yes, well this could mean the rep never called; but this is a feeble excuse because booksellers are regularly sent publishers' lists of forth-coming titles – if they aren't they should have called for them – and have copies of trade publications announcing what is coming out and when. If they haven't heard of your book, they can look it up very quickly and at least offer to order it for you or your friend – provided, that is, he's got the title right or at least remembers the name of the publisher.

The bookseller says they've ordered copies and they haven't arrived; or they were told by the publishers that it was out of print (it isn't): we are now entering the area of genuine and reasonable complaints. So complain to the publisher by all means. But don't forget to tell him which bookshop it was. If you don't, there's noth-ing he can do about it.

If your book hasn't been reviewed or has been ignored in the main and most important literary columns it's seldom any use blaming your publisher. Conceivably he might have neglected to send out sufficient review copies or have sent them too late; but it's a whole lot more likely that out of the great pile of review copies received by the literary editors yours wasn't one of the lucky few to be selected. Some publishers are better at getting their books reviewed than others, but it's a chancy business. No one can oblige a journal to review any given book or even put much pressure on the editor concerned. The publisher will now and then write a persuasive covering letter, but literary editors get shoals of these, too. And if your publisher does succeed in getting a review for your book, it's no guarantee that the review will be a good one!

If you feel like complaining about the review itself, you could write to the journal – not of course complaining that the reviewer didn't like your book and should have, but, if you can, faulting him on inaccuracies or really unfair imputations. With luck this could lead to further correspondence, which is excellent publicity.

Postscript

It does seem that the 'conventional' story-telling novel, which includes most bestsellers in the not-so-distant past, tends to be out of favour today unless by a well-established author, as, rather oddly, do novels about middle-aged, middle-class characters. A publisher who actually liked a novel I sent her recently returned it as lacking sufficient 'pzazz' [*sic*] to be a mass-market bestseller (fair enough) and, rather more alarmingly, 'a little too mid-life to appeal to the younger reader'. I'm not sure where the older readers go for their novels nowadays; maybe to the established names which presumably still sell. This is not a golden rule, I hope, but the trend for first novels is for 'pzazz' to make them stand out, in the publisher's opinion, attracting the famous hype with a mouth-watering and much publicized advance, and the book may go on to greater things or, equally, sink without trace.

Yes, it is a lottery, but that doesn't deter ticket buyers and shouldn't deter first novelists. Provided you follow the 'rules' and present a professional MS or synopsis, which is what this little book is all about, sticking to the Read On Factor, it won't guarantee publication, but it will considerably increase its chances.

I did warn you at the beginning that there would be a number of important things this book wouldn't tell you and gave various reasons. Perhaps with hindsight again they could be reduced to two: because sometimes I don't know the answer; and because there are aspects of writing which I don't believe can be learnt from a book, or tuition or indeed from anyone else – aspects you can learn only the hard way, by experience.

If this handbook has helped to make the hard way a little less hard by glancing at the aspects that *can* be learnt from others – the professional approach – it will have served its purpose. I doubt if it will make you a better writer. I hope it may make you a more professional one and will save time and aggravation – yours, editors', agents' – and enable you to get on with what really counts: the development of your talent.

Good luck!